Every Scene
by Heart:

A Camino de Santiago Memoir

Peri Zahnd

Walking the Camino de Santiago, the ancient five-hundred-mile Christian pilgrim path through Spain, was one of the highlights of my life. I know that it was a gift to me, one I will treasure forever. It came at just the right time, was such an affirmation of God's deep love, and I am forever grateful.

I took a journal with me and even had to buy a second one along the way. I made notes every day about what we did and what was going on in my heart and mind. I knew when I came home that it would be important not only to remember but to very purposefully process the Camino, to extract from it every possible benefit. I needed to savor and fully experience my experiences. I didn't want to just have pleasant memories but to allow the Camino to continue to do its work in me. And so I wrote this book for me, and that would have been enough.

I didn't initially plan to publish my Camino story—there seem to be so many others available. I didn't think the world needed another Camino story. But then I realized that my story is unique because…well, it's my story. I walked the Camino with Brian, my beloved husband, soulmate, and best friend, sharing many beautiful experiences; but at the same time we each walked our own Camino. It seems only right to share with others what was so precious to me. And so I make myself vulnerable and offer a bit of my life to my friends and family and anyone who has ever longed to do something similar. I offer this for those who need to be reminded that God is always with us, to those of you who understand that your life too is a pilgrimage, and for those who need to be encouraged that God will indeed make all things beautiful in their time.

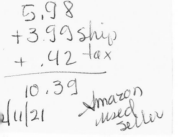

Sundown, yellow moon,
I replay the past,
I know every scene by heart,
They all went by so fast.

—Bob Dylan

Contents

Prologue

"Blessed in the man whose heart is set on pilgrimage....
passing through the Valley of Weeping, they make it a spring....
they go from strength to strength, every one of them appears before God."

Psalm 84: 5,6

lessed is the one whose heart is set on pilgrimage." That proclamation from the psalmist has always thrilled my soul. The excitement of a journey, a long journey filled with the unknown, a sacred journey with a holy goal in mind. Blessed is the one whose heart is set on making the journey with God, traveling with God, traversing one's life with the goal of coming to know God and to be known by God. Blessed is the one who walks with God and trusts that the pain, disappointment, and tears of this life can be transformed into beautiful things.

Brian and I discovered the mountains when we were thirty and our kids were young. We fell in love with them and have vacationed in Colorado every summer since, hiking hundreds of miles through Rocky Mountain National Park. We know those mountains, we love them and call them ours. Hiking is hard work, the opposite of lying on a beach, but though it is taxing to the body, these trips are a rest to our weary souls. Hiking in the mountains is restorative and life-giving.

I love hitting the trail in the early morning carrying a backpack filled with the bare essentials. I love breathing the cool mountain air, smelling the pines. We walk often in silence, my thoughts free to roam, frequently going deep, pondering the mysteries of life, marveling over the mysteries of God. The wide-open spaces of the mountains allow thoughts to be expansive, broad, spacious. There is room to enlarge and grow.

I realized years ago that another reason I love hiking so much is that it is the perfect metaphor for me of the life I'm living. It helps me to make sense of it all, to understand that life really is a journey with much purpose. I feel better connected to my life, connected to the earth, connected to God.

The much-beloved Twenty-third Psalm is another pilgrimage psalm—a psalm about a journey through particular places, rich with imagery. That pilgrim is moving—from green pastures to still waters, walking on paths of righteousness. Someone on a path isn't aimlessly wandering but is walking with purpose and direction with a goal in mind.

That path will take her places she didn't necessarily want to go, through some deep valleys of disappointment, to places of grief and loss, through fearful dark places. And God will always be there, right by her side. She will experience the unexpected, unexplainable comfort and presence of God. She will learn vital lessons, deep truths about life and about who she is. And she, in time, will be transformed along the way. She will learn to trust God and come to have the peace of knowing that everything will turn out perfectly in the end.

I still can't believe I got to go on a real pilgrimage, a dreamed-of pilgrimage, the Camino de Santiago. Sometimes dreams do come true—something you've dreamed of for a long time, and suddenly, it's upon you, it's happening! I often remind myself of this, particularly when I'm going through a hard time, reminding myself that it won't be this way forever, reminding myself of how it feels to long for something for so long and then finally see your dream come to pass. The Psalmist sang that when the captives were released from their long exile and finally allowed to go back to Israel—"We were like those who dream, and then we were filled with laughter, and sang for joy, as the nations all around said, 'What amazing things the Lord has done for them!'" (Psalm 126)

Finally the day came when we were really going to do it, to live our dream. We were going to take a sabbatical—seven weeks away, a week for every five years we'd pastored Word of Life Church. We were going to be gone seven weeks, seven sevens, a Sabbath of weeks, and we were going to see a dream come true, walking the Camino de Santiago for five hundred miles across Spain.

We'd heard about the Camino four years earlier when we watched the movie, *The Way*, with Martin Sheen. At least that's the way Brian tells the story. I kind of think I had heard of it earlier, but the movie definitely brought it to the forefront of our awarenesses. From the moment I saw the film, I longed with all my heart to walk it, all five hundred miles. But I knew it was a pipe dream, it could never happen. We could never be away from our church that long, could we? We had started Word of Life Church when we were so young, just twenty-one and twenty-two, and pastoring it was all we'd done our entire adult lives. We'd labored over it, wept over it, rejoiced over it. We often said the church was our fourth child. We had three sons, and then our daughter, Word of Life, and often joked she had given us more trouble than all the boys put together. We dearly love our church and are very grateful for the opportunity to serve God there.

But this Camino dream wasn't a pipe dream because four years later we were doing it! We were actually going to go! When we saw *The Way* in the midst of the nastiness of the 2012 presidential campaign, Brian had said, "Let's do it in 2016—I can't bear to be in America for another presidential campaign." (Little did either of us know how much uglier that one would turn out to be.)

Scheduling something four years ahead? That's practically impossible for someone who loves impulsivity as much as I do. It seemed like a joke. In fact, I never really thought it would happen. I dutifully wrote it on the calendar, I allowed myself to dream about it and plan for it, I spent countless hours reading numerous books and everything I could find online, but in the back of my mind I prepared myself for disappointment. Early in the spring of 2016 I used the frequent flyer miles I'd carefully saved to reserve our airline tickets, and I only did so with the knowledge that those tickets could be canceled and the miles reused within a year for something else, because I still didn't think we would actually go. As spring turned to summer, I prepared myself to be disappointed. The day would come when we would get real and acknowledge the impossibility. May passed, June passed, and it wasn't until July that something in my heart opened up and I began to believe that this might really happen and allowed myself to start getting excited.

The day had come and we were leaving, flying to Paris on the fifteenth anniversary of September 11 right after Sunday morning church. Our bags were packed—oh so carefully! The cat was sent off (and returned the day we left but that's another story.) Our church had a sending-off party for us on Friday night, and I treasured the pile of notes and prayers that I took home. I sat and read them all early the next morning and wanted to take them with me, but wisdom said no, as it had also said no to every other non-essential. I picked out a few representative ones anyhow and tucked them inside my small journal. The journey had begun…

To come to the pleasure you have not
You must go by a way in which you enjoy not.
To come to the knowledge you have not
You must go by a way in which you know not.
To come to the possession you have not
You must go by a way in which you possess not.
To come to be what you are not
You must go by a way in which you are not.

St. John of the Cross
Spain, 16th century

St. Joseph, Missouri to St. Jean Pied de Port, France

*W*e arrived in Paris early in the morning, went through Passport Control, collected our luggage, and made our way to the RER station, the train that's connected to the subway, but is not the subway. Exiting the terminal, you take a train to get to the train, which is also not the subway, but the train that connects the terminals. Confusing, I know, but we'd been in Paris before, used the RER to get from the airport to the city, and I'd very carefully and painstakingly researched every move we had to make.

Finally arriving at the train station with luggage in tow, we studied the RER map until finding the stop Antony where we needed to get off to arrive at Orly, the domestic airport on the other side of Paris. The RER didn't travel all the way to Orly, but there was supposed to be a shuttle we could catch at this particular stop. I knew all these details, but just to make sure I approached the information desk and was relieved when told, in flawless English, that to get to Orly we needed to take the RER to

Antony where we could catch a shuttle…..just like I already knew. We then joined a long line to buy tickets, found our train, boarded, and we were off. An hour later we arrived at Antony and found that the shuttle was not a bus, as I'd imagined, but another train which quickly whisked us away to the Orly airport. Modern mass transit is amazing. In less than twenty-four hours we would drive forty miles from our home to the Kansas City airport, fly to Chicago, transfer terminals via train, fly to Paris, transfer airports via three different trains, fly to Biarritz, and then take a taxi to the hotel I'd reserved. I thought about the fact that the speed of life was going to slow down a whole lot very soon! If we had wanted to, within those twenty-four hours, we could also have taken the train from Biarritz to St. Jean-Pied-de-Port where we would start our walk. But I wisely figured that last leg would probably be a little too much to handle and besides, I wanted to be awake to enjoy it, so we saved it for the next day.

Besides all the shuttles and trains, modern airports utilize a lot of escalators and moving sidewalks. I can't help but think of the Jetsons, one of my favorite childhood television cartoons, when I'm at one of these big international airports. Checking our luggage at Orly was definitely a Jetsons moment. You approach a giant unmanned box, place your piece of luggage in a compartment, slide a plastic door closed over it, and then scan your boarding pass. Lights blink, there are some electronic beeps, and then WHOOSH! The door slides open and the compartment is empty. Magic. Your bag has just blasted off to some unknown destination—you can only hope to see it again when you reach your destination. We did it again for the second piece of luggage. I wanted to video the spectacle but with Brian's encouragement I was able to restrain myself.

We napped through the next flight. It was a relief to know that we had a hotel waiting for us as soon as we arrived in Biarritz, and when we got there around 4:00 we laid down and relaxed for a few minutes, glad the travel was over. But not for long—you have to work to reset your internal clock and overcome jetlag. The best way to do that is with sunlight and some physical activity. So we went out to see the city and find someplace to eat dinner.

Our hotel was across the street from the train station, extremely convenient. Our train to St. Jean-Pied-de-Port left shortly after 11:00 so the next morning after breakfast at the hotel we went to see about buying tickets and to try to figure out what track the train would come in on. Trains in Europe can be very confusing. We got our tickets and then went back to get our packs.

We'd packed them the night before after arriving at the hotel. We had brought suitcases on this trip, old suitcases I planned to abandon. Our packs were inside them, partially packed, with the remainder of the stuff loose in the suitcase. I'd read that packs can get damaged as checked luggage, particularly the ultralights we were hiking with. And I'd actually experienced this a couple of years ago, not realizing until I was beginning a hike in the Rocky Mountains that the waist strap and clip on my pack were sheared off, remembering then that I hadn't used the pack since flying home from the mountains the previous summer. (Fortunately our son Philip was with us—Philip the rock climber, who spent a few of his teenage years with a rope in his hand practicing the various knots required in serious mountaineering. He fashioned a handy way to clip and unclip so that I was able to use the pack on that vacation and then get it repaired when I got home.) Our packs had been safe nestled in the suitcases, and as we checked out of the hotel, I mentioned to the desk clerk, "Those suitcases in our room? We meant to leave them there." That was a good feeling, already beginning to shed some baggage!

We walked across the street to the train station with our packs on our back. Were we finally really beginning? I felt so excited! We walked down the stairs and crossed under the various platforms and came up on Platform 3, about twenty minutes before our train was scheduled to depart. There was only a few people waiting and we sat down on a bench. A young woman sat nearby, probably in her early twenties, and she too had a backpack.

"So, are you here to walk the Camino de Santiago?" I said, trying to be friendly.

"Duh, yeah, me and every other person who's getting on this train." She told me she was from Germany, and just then a train pulled up. Was this our train? I wondered to myself. (I didn't think I wanted to show my stupidity to this girl who seemed to know so much!) Brian and I looked at one another and he said, "I guess this is our train," as the little crowd on the platform had grown to maybe twenty or thirty people, most of whom had backpacks and were beginning to board. Everyone seemed to be very quiet and I realize now that we may have all shared the same sense of nervousness and anticipation. In fact, the comment I interpreted as somewhat cold I now think was probably masking that anxiety. German Train Girl turned out to be a very decent, interesting person. You can't always trust first impressions.

Having found a seat, we all sat in silence, Brian and I occasionally whispering to one another. It was really a different vibe than I've experienced on trains or planes or any kind of public transport. Everyone was very serious, not reading or chatting, just sitting. Finally, the doors shut and my heart began to race as the train pulled out from the station. We were off! (Brian did lean over and whisper to me that the train pulled out at exactly 11:10 as scheduled, not only to the minute, but to the second. This impressed him greatly. I, however, did not even know a watch could be set to the second. These things do not impress me nearly as much, which is just one small way of the many in which we see life very differently.)

It was a picturesque hour, not high-speed this time, but a gentle rolling ride through woods, past streams, and into the Pyrenees Mountains. I had a sense that as we moved forward on the tracks, we were moving back in time, that some bit of magic was transforming our train, like the Polar Express. We would be arriving at a place where time, in fact, had slowed way down, where time maybe even occasionally stood still, and certainly didn't really matter much at all, on the magical Camino de Santiago. Finally the train pulled up and stopped at our destination, St. Jean-Pied-de-Port. There was the sound of the hydraulic whoosh as the doors opened, and then all was quiet. The people stood up quietly, hoisted their packs, and silently got off the train, crossed the platform, and began to walk up the street.

"Where do we go? What do we do?" Our only choice was to follow the crowd, who seemed somehow to know. And in perhaps ten minutes we found ourselves at the Pilgrim Office. Somehow we arrived there before most of the people on the train, and a few minutes later we were invited to a desk where a smiling woman who spoke almost no English began to register us as *peregrinos* (the Spanish word for pilgrim). She took our names and pertinent information and issued us a *credencial*, a pilgrim passport. She instructed us to get it stamped everywhere we stayed and that stamps were also available at churches, some restaurants, and bars along the way. There were sixty spots for stamps on the *credencial* which meant we had room for one or two every day. (We ended our Caminos with a stamp in every spot which required a bit of planning toward the end.)

She also gave us a list of *albergues*, the lodging places exclusively for pilgrims along the way, usually dormitory sleeping. We had already made up our minds we would spend some of our nights in hotels as we both agreed that too much sleeping in dorms might make us a little crazy. And pilgrims in medieval times did not sleep exclusively in *albergues* or hostels—they took advantage of whatever accommodations were available. The last part of her instruction was a map of the first stage of the Camino, the route over the Pyrenees. It was considered to be the hardest day of the entire Camino—twenty-five kilometers, over fifteen miles, with a lot of elevation loss and gain. I had been simultaneously looking forward to and dreading this day for a long time. A fifteen-mile hike in the mountains wasn't daunting—in fact, I'd done two of those earlier in the summer in the Rockies. But I wasn't used to carrying a twenty-pound pack in the Rockies. And it was this stage, the very first day, in the Martin Sheen film on the Camino, *The Way*, that a man had died!

Now the plan all along had been to travel to St. Jean on Tuesday, find a place to stay, and begin early the next morning. But I'd secretly been wondering if we could jumpstart that and had finally suggested it to Brian as a possibility the day before. As an Enneagram Seven personality I always like to keep my possibilities open until the last possible moment and so I hadn't mentioned it until then. I knew there was an *albergue* located ten kilometers up the mountain road. Ten kilometers (6.2 miles) is kind of ridiculously short for a day on the Camino. But what if we called it a half day? What if we actually started this afternoon and stayed there? So I mentioned the plan to the woman registering us. I "mentioned" it by pointing to the *albergue* on the list she had just given us and then realizing I actually knew how to say in Spanish, "Can you make a reservation for me?" "*Puede hacer una reservación para mi, por favor? Para esta noche.*"

I had spent a few hours, a very few hours, listening to Spanish language CDs in my car, and that was one of the very few phrases I had learned. It turned out to be very handy, but a few other phrases would have been really handy, too. We both knew precious little Spanish. Our registrar kindly picked up the phone and made a call, spoke for a minute in rapid Spanish, hung up, smiled in a sad sort of way, and then said, "*No. Es complet.*" *Complet.* That was another word we learned fairly quickly. Full. No room. Bummer.

But then she pointed to the map and communicated that there was another possibility, not ten kilometers away, but just six. Six kilometers, less than four miles. Not far, but it would be four miles we wouldn't have to do tomorrow. Eleven miles rather than fifteen was not at all daunting and seemed to relieve the anxiety I felt. And we were both so ready to get started! We quickly agreed, she made a phone call, and we had a reservation.

The last step of our registration process was the explanation of a map of the route, and she pointed out there were two routes— the Napoleon route over the mountains and the road route down below which skirted the mountain. Of course we were going over the mountain, there was no question. The main point of her explanation, however, was towards the end of the hike, the descent. She pointed out there were two ways down and made a big red X over the left route. No! She was emphatic, repeating the instruction, tracing the X over and over. Why couldn't we go that way? I had no idea but we shook our heads yes, we understood, because there was no way to actually ask why.

She then led us over to a basket of scallop shells with twine attached. We were to choose one and tie it to our packs, identifying us now as *peregrinos* on the Camino. Scallop shells have long been identified with the Camino, a reminder of the beach where the boat carrying the remains of Santiago (St. James) landed. She then pointed to the door, indicated we were to go to the left, and said, "*Buen camino.*" We went out, looked both ways, and then plopped down on a bench right outside the door. Yes, we were ready to start, but not that very minute! We tied our shells on our packs and stowed our *credencials* and other paperwork away. We took a few deep breaths, realized it was past lunchtime, and saw a little café not ten feet away. It looked as good as anywhere so we went in. We ate some delicious *bocadillos con jamón* (bo-ca-DEE-yos) a.k.a. ham sandwiches. I enjoyed the three friendly young people running the café who were happily singing along with the music playing, reminding me of hanging out with the youth group at church camp a few months before. We got coffee afterwards and relaxed a bit.

"Ready to go?" Brian asked.

"Well, yeah, but don't you want to see the village here a bit?" So we walked down the main street of that charming medieval village, a pedestrian pathway lined with shops and *albergues* and restaurants. But our hearts really weren't into exploring St. Jean-Pied-de-Port, they were feeling the magnetic pull of Santiago. It was irresistible—so we gave in, turned around and headed in the direction of the Camino. We'll have to go back another time.

We quickly began to see the yellow *flechas* (arrows) that would mark our way, along with the blue signs with yellow scallop shells and various other markers. We were off to see the wizard, following the yellow brick road. Our hearts were filled with joy, excitement, and expectation of good things to come. The road was immediately very steep! And I hadn't realized how hot it was. But the beauty we were beholding caused us not to care. We crossed a small river on a beautiful bridge with lovely old homes and buildings on both sides, another ancient stone bridge just a few hundred feet away. The dwellings on the road grew further and further apart as we left the town behind us. A woman rode by on a bicycle and said *"Buen camino."* Even that was thrilling!

The day had started off beautiful and sunny but suddenly clouded up and fifteen minutes into our walk it surprisingly began to rain. We hadn't expected to be getting out our raincoats and our pack covers so soon, but we did in a hurry! It rained moderately hard for maybe five minutes, abruptly stopped, and the sun came out again. We stopped to take the raincoats off and continued our steep ascent. I saw cows! Not just any cows, but picturesque cows, pretty blonde cows, cows with bells! They were eating beautiful golden hay. I took pictures. Lots of pictures. "Brian, look at those beautiful cows!"

The road wound around and became even steeper. There were cows right out in the road, oblivious to us, milling about, doing what cows do. I took a picture of Brian with a cow. We weren't in a hurry, we only had six kilometers to go, and we enjoyed every minute. But yes, it was steep, and the rain had made it so humid we were sweating profusely and drinking lots of water. Suddenly six kilometers was about as far as I wanted to go, and when we finally reached the *albergue,* we had caught up and passed three women hiking together, moving much slower than we were and seeming to have a tough time of it. They weren't finished either, as they had reservations at the further *albergue*—four more hot, steep kilometers away. I was very grateful that we hadn't been able to go there after all, realizing I was still experiencing fatigue from jetlag.

We entered the *albergue* where a woman greeted us in French. And I was able to say in French, "We have a reservation." I took four years of high school French and rarely get to use it. My skills are only rudimentary but far better than my almost non-existent Spanish. Tomorrow we would cross over into Spain so this was my first and last opportunity to speak French. I gave her our names and then boldly asked if perhaps she had a private room. Really, I felt very lucky to have a reservation at all but I decided there was no reason not to ask. She didn't respond but turned her attention to another couple who had walked in, and they entered into a lengthy conversation I couldn't comprehend. I felt a little confused, but finally she beckoned us both to follow her out the door, down the drive, and across the road to a completely different building, into a dormitory where she showed the other couple their bunks. I was expecting her to point out which ones we were to sleep in, but she took us to a small private room with our own bath and an outside door! I was thrilled and glad my assertiveness had paid off.

We showered and then washed our sweaty clothes in the bathroom sink, hanging them outside to dry. Supper wasn't served until 7:00 and it looked like another storm was blowing in.

And blow in it did, with a vengeance! Within half an hour we were bringing our still-wet laundry inside to continue drying. The rain began to fall hard and the trees bent to and fro as they wrestled with an unseen force. We sat and watched the storm through the open door of our room until the wind changed and we had to close it to stay dry. It seemed to match the intense euphoria I'd felt all day—energy, aliveness. I loved watching it, but I would have hated being in it, and I thought about the three slow-moving women we'd seen on the road and prayed for them. God, I hope they've arrived, take care of them, help them. I prayed for anyone else who might be out in it and thanked God fervently that I wasn't. The storm raged on for a couple of hours but finally abated right before 7:00, when dinner was scheduled in the main house where we'd registered. We were able to walk outside and across the road without getting wet. The storm had spent itself like a child who'd screamed and raged until she was exhausted and now could only whimper.

We entered the dining room where one very long table was set for twenty people or so and found seats. Like the train, everyone was pretty quiet, coming in by twos or threes or alone, but soon the table was full. It was full of strangers who didn't quite know what to say or how to break the ice or even if the person sitting next to them spoke their language—it was awkward. Everyone there was probably just beginning their Camino and was a little uptight. The ice broke slowly with eye contact and shy smiles, and when the food was carried in, we graduated to words and gestures, "Can you pass the bread, *por favor*?"

The food was very good—a port aperitif, then a starter of vegetable soup which we ladled up from big tureens, followed by roast chicken with tomatoes and red peppers. I learned that the two women sitting across from me were French, a mother and daughter. The mother looked quite elderly, surprisingly old to be walking the Camino, and was silent throughout the meal. The daughter spoke some English and explained they were only going as far as Pamplona. Only Pamplona? I wondered. We expected to reach there on the third day! This was the beginning of my understanding of the myriad number of ways people walk the Camino. Some just do tiny sections at a time—particularly Europeans who don't have to travel far to be in Northern Spain. They spend a few days or a week to walk and then come back at a future date to do another installment, starting where they left off. I talked to many who were doing that—some who said they expect to finish in, "oh, maybe seven years? Maybe 2023?" It made me very grateful we have the opportunity and time to come and walk the entire Camino—oh God, may it happen!

A Danish man across the table spoke good English. His name was Gert, and he was walking the Camino for a second time. I told him we didn't know any Danes except for Soren Kierkegaard, the important existentialist philosopher and writer who has been a big influence on Brian. In fact, he'd just read a brand new biography on him a few weeks ago, and I'd read the first few chapters before I'd abandoned it to come on this trip. He looked blankly at us and said, "I don't know who you're talking about."

A Dane who doesn't know Kierkegaard? Brian mentioned a few book titles and he just shook his head. This was becoming another awkward moment, so we changed the subject. Several minutes passed, and then Gert said, "You don't perhaps mean 'Care-Key-Go,' do you?"

"Care-Key-Go? Uh, is that how you say it?" Yes, we'd so Anglicized his name that he couldn't understand who we were talking about.

"Well, of course I know Care-Key-Go. Every Dane knows Care-Key-Go! And Hans Christian Anderson." We had a little laugh about the misunderstanding and continued to talk together as we enjoyed an apple tart served with cheese and jam. We were finished with dinner now but lingering when someone said, "Look at the rainbow!" The entire group jumped up to go to the large window and then out on to the big porch outside. It had remained dark and cloudy after the thunderstorm but now, just at the hour of sunset, the sun had popped out and a glorious, vibrant double rainbow had appeared over the mountains. All the pilgrims were snapping pictures and milling about, finally relaxed and talking easily. We met people who'd been sitting at the other end of the table and talked about what had brought us there, our hopes and desires for the Camino. Finally, we went off to bed, our bodies and spirits both having been satisfied by the wonderful meal and the joy of connecting with others beginning the same journey.

It was a beautiful evening. The storm had cooled things off considerably. We had been watching the weather for weeks, and it had been unusually hot this summer and fall. As it turned out, this storm broke the long hot spell and for that I was exceedingly grateful. I had been dreading walking in the heat Spain had been experiencing. We went to bed with the outside door to our room open. There was a full moon that night and the wind from the storm hadn't quite died down. It was playful, even sassy, making the trees outside sway and dance, silhouetted by the moon behind them. The curtain at the door danced as well. The wind seemed to be showing its power, implying it could do so much more—it made me rejoice in the glory and majesty of both Creation and Creator. I lay awake for quite a while in the night, my heart full, overwhelmed with gratitude and excitement about what might lie ahead. I was enjoying the moment so much I didn't want to go to sleep, but thankfully my body knew better, and in the morning I awoke rested and ready to go.

Over the Pyrenees

Our hostess, or *hospitalera*, had announced breakfast would be served at 7:00 and so we were up, dressed, and standing in line at the door in the dark ready to go when she unlocked it. We chatted easily with the other pilgrims until the door opened and we were ushered into the dining room. We sat down to the table where pitchers of hot coffee, tea, and orange juice were waiting. As soon as we were seated, plates piled high with thick slices of toast were brought out. There were several kinds of marmalade and honey. I had coffee and a piece of toast but after the meal last night I wisely now knew to save space for the second course. I had visions of platters of steaming scrambled eggs and thick pieces of bacon. I waited patiently but when others pushed away from the table and began to leave it finally dawned on me that this was it. Spain is part of "the continent"—welcome to a continental breakfast! And so began our first real day on the Camino, as yesterday had just been a head start.

We started up the road with headlamps and enthusiasm. The headlamps were soon turned off, but the enthusiasm remained. We walked up, up, up on the steep roadway. It was even steeper than the day before, a winding road past flocks of sheep with the soothing sound of their bells, an idyllic mountain vista that was timeless and unchanged for hundreds of years except for the occasional car that passed by. We climbed slowly, the beauty that was everywhere—mountains, trees, clouds, fields and flocks— distracting us from the difficulty of the climb. We were never really alone, but other *peregrinos* surrounded us—those who'd stayed where we had, but also those who had just left St. Jean early this morning, as well as those staying at the *albergue* that had been full when we tried to get a reservation. I was surprised late in the morning when I realized I didn't recognize any of the people I'd met last night around us—they were either ahead or behind, and we had a brand new group of companions. That was to be our experience for the next several weeks—companions who were forever changing just as the scenery was also changing.

The elevation gain from St. Jean-Pied-de-Port to the top of the mountains is almost 4,000 feet and then down steeply to Roncesvalles another 1,600 feet. I love being up high in the mountains, higher than the trees, under such a big, big sky, breathing fresh air and soaking up the sunshine. It was a beautiful day. We were carrying sandwiches from the *albergue* as we knew there would be nothing to buy along the way but were surprised when we came upon a food truck. They were selling drinks and snacks and big hunks of Manchego cheese—sheep cheese that is indigenous to the region, a delicious hard cheese with a nutty flavor. *Peregrinos* were sitting around on the ground enjoying a break. I saw a familiar face, "Hey Care-Key-Go!"

My new friend turned around, gave me a big smile, and shared his cheese. Brian returned from having just bought some and we now had more than we could all eat, sharing the sandwiches as well. And when we started walking again, Care-Key-Go walked with us. I asked him about having walked the Camino earlier and he told us his story.

He'd lost his wife when he was sixty-five, three years earlier, and said he was crazy with grief. He couldn't do anything, just sat in his house. After a year, his daughter said, "Dad, you've got to get out and do something. Why don't you go walk the Camino de Santiago?" And so he did. He said it helped him, helped him a lot. Two months after returning home, he realized his time there wasn't finished and went back and volunteered for a month at an *albergue*, helping other *peregrinos* on their journeys. Now he was back to walk it again. It had evidently made a significant impact on him.

We chatted about other things and I brought up the movie *Babette's Feast*, a favorite of ours that is set in Denmark. The movie is about a religious group that lives a very austere and legalistic lifestyle. He was familiar with it and told me his wife was raised in that religion—the black Christians, he called them. It's not a racial designation but a reference to the plain black clothing that they all wear. "She got out as soon as she could." He told me he didn't believe in God, at least the Christian God. He believed in the "old gods," the gods of nature. Then he told me of a memorable experience he had had recently while out in some woods of being overwhelmed with a sense of gratitude. "I just said thank you—I'm not sure to who." He told me that while on the

Camino he went to every church service he could; he found them to be beautiful and they deeply touched something in him. But he wanted to reiterate that he didn't "believe."

We continued to cross the Pyrenees. The day could not have been more beautiful; the temperature was perfect and the sun was shining. My heart was happy and light. I rejoiced that we were doing this today and not yesterday in the storm. I had been fearful of this day (because of all the hype about how hard it was) but it turned out to be delightful. Finally the path turned downward into the steep descent. Very soon we identified the fork we'd been warned not to take, still not knowing why. Was the path washed out or impassable? Brian wanted to take it but I convinced him to follow the rules and do as we'd been told. The winding path we took was steep enough—down, down, down. We saw the huge monastery of Roncesvalles which had been converted into an *albergue* when we were still high above it, and eventually we arrived.

I had enjoyed talking with Gert; he was a very kind, thoughtful man. I found it interesting that he didn't want to believe, but yet it was walking an ancient Christian pilgrim route that pulled him out of his intractable grief. And that he loved going to the Catholic mass—attracted by beauty. I looked forward to talking more to him in the days to come and was surprised and a bit sad that I never saw him again after that day. But that's the Camino. I prayed several times for him as the weeks passed.

All my fears about "the hardest day of the Camino," the crossing of the Pyrenees, were unfounded. I had loved the day and it didn't seem any harder than many of our days in Rocky Mountain National Park. We went inside and were instructed to take our shoes off and leave them in the "shoe room," joining a line to be assigned a bed. I remember how it hurt to walk on the stone floor barefoot; my feet were really sore, probably from the weight of my pack. When we finally were able to register, I once again asked about the "private room"—it had worked yesterday. The man, an American volunteer, just laughed and said, "Honey, you're on the Camino! Forget about private rooms!" We were assigned beds #253 and #254 and climbed slowly to the second floor to find them, every step hurting my bare feet.

The *albergue* had been recently remodeled. It was still a huge room filled with bunk beds, but dividers had been added forming cubicles for four people. Brian and I shared a bunk bed and he generously took the top bunk. Across from me was Jeff, a 60-year old Aussie, and on the top bunk was Guy, a 20-year old Israeli from Tel Aviv—(a thoroughly modern, secular Jewish kid walking an ancient Christian pilgrim route?) Both were doing the Camino solo.

We took some time unpacking, getting organized and showering. I'd been warned there was no hot water but the rumor was unfounded. The restroom facilities were adequate and clean. It was cold in the *albergue* and I was happy to get inside my sleeping bag to rest for a bit. Afterwards we went out for coffee. I had been lamenting just a few hours earlier that I was carrying two coats—a fleece jacket and a packable down jacket, but I put them both on when we went out into the town, necessitated by a combination of falling temperatures and the post-hike chill I always experience in the mountains. I was very glad to have them and would wear both together many times in the weeks to come.

What else was in that heavy bag I'd carried so far that made my feet and hips ache so? Yes, there was a slow dawning, a gradual awareness coming to me that the day had been harder than I'd wanted to admit. What was I carrying? Well, some Merrill flip-flops for wearing after hiking and also a very light pair of sneakers that were soft and cushy and soothing to my feet. I was so happy each afternoon to take off my otherwise beloved LaSportiva trail runners and put them on. I had bought the LaSportivas three years earlier, and they'd been the best hiking shoes I'd ever owned. I tried to replace them so I could start with a new pair but the style had changed and I didn't like the new ones nearly as well. I was stuck trying to make up my mind between the old beloved and the new not-so-beloved and had decided a week before we left to go with the tried and true. But then Caleb, my oldest son, a long distance runner, looked at them and said, "Mom, these shoes don't have five hundred miles left in them." I explained how hard I had tried to replace them and three minutes later he had located a brand-new identical pair on eBay. I quickly ordered them with expedited shipping and gave thanks to God (and to Caleb) for this provision.

So I had three pairs of shoes. I needed them! As for clothing, I had two identical pairs of lightweight, quick-drying hiking pants— one black and one blue. And two identical lightweight, quick-drying long-sleeve hooded t-shirts—one orange and one teal. I also had a third pair of pants to wear afternoons and evenings with a warmer long-sleeved t-shirt. This was recommended and I was happy to carry them—it's not always possible to wash clothes every day and I have a strong aversion to wearing dirty clothes. Brian only had two pair and he actually went to dinner one night wearing my pajama pants because both of his were in the laundry. Uh, pajama pants? Yes, I had to have something to sleep in, especially in a dorm—pajama pants and a t-shirt, which I also wore a few warm afternoons. And Brian wore my pajama pants to dinner? Yes, they were grey and didn't look too bad except that they were several inches too short for him. But it's amazing how you really don't care about things like that on the Camino!

I also had a Kindle. A sleeping bag. A sleeping bag liner. (I loved it!) A raincoat. (In hindsight, too bulky. I should have gotten a lighter one but I've had this one for fifteen years or more, worn it in the mountains so many times, and I'm sentimental about it.) And it turns out that water is heavy but unfortunately necessary. Somehow all these things added up to twenty pounds. I didn't purge anything once I was on the Camino. I could have dumped a thing or two, lost a tiny bit of weight, but sentimentality and thriftiness restrained me.

We both also carried walking poles, as did the majority of pilgrims. They take a tremendous strain off your joints and can avert a fall. I never regretted having poles—they were my constant companions.

The *albergue* in Roncesvalles is the largest on the Camino with accommodations for several hundred people. Arriving around 2:00, we were given bunks on the third floor as the second floor was already filled. When the third floor was filled people were assigned to the basement, and those arriving later yet slept in what sounded to me like converted shipping containers. The person relating this story had not been happy about it and said they had not had a comfortable night. I appreciate the efforts, however, to accommodate pilgrims and not just turn them away. There are all sorts of *albergues*—municipal and church-sponsored and private for-profit. The range of accommodations, too, is huge—from primitive to well-appointed, clean to not so clean, old to new. There are even a few that don't have electricity or running water.

We had bought tickets for dinner and there were two seatings—7:00 and 8:30. I couldn't imagine waiting to eat until 8:30 and was glad we didn't have to. We all waited in line and at 7:00 were allowed to enter a huge dining room. Brian and I sat down at a big round table filled with mostly German speakers. I tried to make friendly conversation with the woman next to me whose eyes got wider and wider until she finally blurted out, "I don't speak good English." So I left her alone and she talked with enthusiasm, in German, to the woman on the other side of her. Brian talked to the man next to him. His large hoop earrings caused us to refer to him as The Pirate—we'd see him often. The food was good; the atmosphere was slightly awkward, but it didn't matter. We were looking forward to the "Pilgrim Blessing Service" at 8:00 at the church.

I had no idea how many pilgrims would turn out for that but was pleasantly surprised; the church was full. The service began when three priests entered singing in Spanish. The entire service was in Spanish, naturally, and I didn't understand a word of it. I wondered if this was what a Catholic Church felt like to most people prior to Vatican II when the services were conducted in Latin. Of course, growing up in it and being there week after week a person would become familiar…these were my musings. No, I didn't understand a word until the very end when the oldest priest who had not yet spoken said in perfect English that everyone was invited to the Communion table, unless, of course, you were not Catholic.

This stunned me. I was not expecting to hear that. It reminded me of a time when I was refused Communion at a Catholic mass. I'll never forget what that rejection felt like, and my mind went back to that day a few years ago…

…I'd gone to see the nuns, my friends, at a nearby monastery. I was going through a tough time and I found myself needing some solace, some peace. I'd never taken communion at a Catholic mass, in fact hadn't been to too many of them, but I'd been encouraged that although it's part of official church policy that only Roman Catholics can take communion, I wouldn't be questioned, but welcomed. We'd become friends with these nuns after they read Brian's book *Unconditional?* and he was invited to come speak to them, the beginning of an ongoing friendship.

In the 11:00 mass I attended that day, the priest moved throughout the people, bringing communion to them as many were elderly and had difficulty walking. I was seated near the back and had my eyes closed but could hear him speaking the words, "The body of Christ," as he approached each person. I sensed him move in front of me and opened my eyes. My hands were already open expectantly, in the "proper" way. However, instead of hearing the words, "The body of Christ," I heard him whisper, "Are you Catholic?"

Busted. I felt a hot flush of embarrassment come over me. I looked him in the eyes and mouthed the only thing I felt I could say, "No." He smiled—compassionately? Or was it condescendingly? He took a step back, waved his hand in front of me, giving me a "blessing" that didn't feel like a blessing, and moved on.

Sister Paula was following behind with the chalice. She hadn't seen what had happened. She held it out and looked inquiringly at me. I shook my head no. I was sad. I was shamed. She would happily have served me, but what good is the blood without the body? And I didn't want to get her in any trouble.

After mass we went to lunch. I sat with Sister Paula and Sister Audrey and the priest, who was very young. Sister Paula introduced me as "Pastor Peri" from Word of Life Church. I never use that title, and she never calls me that, but I think she was making a point to the priest. She told him about Brian and how much she loved us. He was pleasant to visit with and very interested in hearing our story. I told him he looked to be about the age of my boys. He told me he was thirty-one and had been a priest for only two months. He was just following the rules. I don't blame him, but I never want anyone to feel what I felt that day—excluded, unworthy, unclean. I know many of my Catholic friends feel the same way I do. And I acknowledge that Protestant and particularly Evangelical churches have their own huge problems. God help us all.

But I do delight in the fact that we practice open Communion at Word of Life Church. All are welcome. Every service is an invitation to come to Jesus, to receive Jesus, to be filled with Jesus. We follow the table practices of Jesus, who welcomed all at his table, even those who were "sinners." Every Sunday this invitation to the communion table is given:

This is the table, not of the church but of the Lord
It is made ready for those who love him and for those who want to love him more
So come, you have much faith, and you who have little
You who have tried to follow, and you who have failed
You who have been here often, and you who have not been here long
Come, for it is the Lord who invites you
It is his will that those who want him should meet him here.

And so what did I do on that evening in Roncesvalles on the Camino de Santiago when the invitation to the Communion table was given? Well, I chose, and hopefully with a right heart, to ignore the comment of the priest and went forward to receive anyhow. I wanted the blood and body of Christ—I needed that strength and grace. Of course, I would not have done anything to cause a scene or be obnoxious. But I had a strong sense of hearing the invitation of Jesus so loud and clear that it drowned out the words of that priest. I must add, now that we've finished the Camino, that this was the one and only time that I felt unwelcome at the Communion table of all the many times we were served Holy Eucharist. I felt there were many churches that went out of their way to be welcoming, and I'm very grateful for that. The Body of Christ is continuing to be healed of its wounds of division.

After church it was time for bed. Preparations were made for the morning, water bottles filled, clothes laid out. We had our phone charger plugged into the outlet near the floor between the two bunk beds as did Guy, the Israeli. We discovered ours had gotten stepped on and broken which was unfortunate as we'd decided to only bring one between the two of us. Guy kindly said we were free to use his when he was done. After the lights were turned off in the entire *albergue* promptly at ten, he remained sitting on the floor with his phone, about two feet away from Jeff's head on the pillow. A few minutes later Jeff said, "About ready to wrap it up, buddy?" "Yeah, in a minute." It made me smile in the dark, grandpa and the young'un—the generation gap is the same around the world. That was the last I remember before I was asleep and dead to the world.

Roncesvalles to Zubiri

I slept like a rock for two hours and then I was awake for three. Jetlag. But I didn't mind as I was so filled with joy and memories of the day and everything that had gotten us here. I had such a sense of God's goodness and an awareness of the beauty of life even with all its imperfections. In fact, I basked in the joy of the imperfections themselves—I mean, why do humans snore? It's a ridiculous trait, accomplishing nothing but annoying people around you. But these pilgrims did snore and I giggled to myself listening as I walked past all those rows of partitions on my way to the bathroom. I loved all those snorers, every one of them.

I rejoiced in the way everything had seemed to come together for us to have such a beautiful experience crossing the Pyrenees. Getting the last minute reservation was perfect. The fact that the further *albergue* was full and the closer one available. Dodging the storm the way we did. The fact that the storm had broken the heat wave. I heard that vans from the *albergues* went out and "rescued" pilgrims caught in it the day before. That would have been a big disappointment as Brian and I shared a goal of not being in any mechanical transport from the time we left St. Jean till we reached Santiago. (We made an exception for elevators—they only go up and down.) A few weeks later we would talk to a couple who had flown from London that day, and their plane was diverted hours away due to the storm. They had to rent a car and drive through the night in order to start on time, having booked hotels for the entire trip. None of this affected us. I was so happy about that but realized at the same time that other people had a very different story. It occurred to me, and this was profound, that "another story" was precisely the answer. Other people had other stories and our situation might have been different; if so, we would have another story, too. And we could tell that story, perhaps of being "caught in a crazy storm but God rescued us and it turned out all right." This was something I've continued to ponder and to marvel at, a gift from the Camino in the form of new revelation and understanding of grace.

I thought, too, about Jeff's final comments to me right before the lights went out. He said he was worried about the world, that we humans had two big problems we were going to have to face— an intolerance of others and extreme greed. The rich were getting richer and the poor were getting poorer and that always leads to revolution. I had to agree with him. This is a scary time for our world, but we need to hold tight to God and truth and each other and believe that, in the words of Martin Luther King, Jr., "The arc of the moral universe is long, but it bends toward justice."

I finally got back to sleep around 3:00 but was awake when the lights went on at 6:00 and we all got up and began to make preparations to leave. All except Guy, however, still snoozing on the top bunk across from me. He was still in bed when we left and that made me giggle again—he wasn't too far past being a teenager. That was the last time I ever saw Guy or Jeff. But I think about these people whose lives intertwined with mine, for just a little bit, and I pray the Camino touched their lives as deeply as it touched mine.

We were on the trail with our headlamps and raincoats by 6:45. It had rained in the night but had mostly stopped and I think any rain that fell on us was actually dripping off the trees overhead as we walked on a path through the woods. Three kilometers down the road we found a crowded café serving breakfast to *peregrinos*. There had been a breakfast offered at the *albergue* for five euros each but we declined to buy tickets. We'd been told that it was crowded, took a long time, and the food wasn't very good. But we also declined because we had very little cash! We had intended to use our credit cards a lot like we do at home and get money from ATM machines as needed. But the first two night's lodging didn't take credit cards, either for the room or for the meals, and there were no ATM machines in the Pyrenees! Our small cash stash was nearly depleted. In fact, we had just about ten euros left and used most of it for breakfast at the café—coffee, orange juice, and a chocolate croissant. I figured when you were going to be walking that far carrying those packs that a chocolate croissant was a justifiable breakfast choice, since the scrambled eggs I would have preferred were unavailable. Our goals for the day were to find an ATM machine and a new phone charger. According to Google, there was an ATM in the next village.

We had ditched the raincoats after breakfast, strolling into the next village about 9:00, and found it to be very, very quiet. Not a single store or business was open, even though this wasn't a tiny town. There was absolutely no one out anywhere—it was like a ghost town. And this was to be the pattern for the weeks to come. I guess when you don't eat dinner till 10:00 or 11:00 at night you don't get up very early in the morning. Fortunately, we did find an ATM machine and rejoiced that we would indeed be eating lunch. We crossed a small stream on a bridge and were once again in farmland. It was a beautiful, peaceful day of walking through the countryside and a couple of villages and we arrived at our destination in Zubiri a little before 2:00. There was a place to stay that looked fine with a sign on the door to ring the buzzer, which we did. A woman finally answered and when we asked about a room, she responded *"Reservación? No? Complet!"* Oh. That word again. They were full.

We stood in the middle of the bridge, an ancient Camino bridge that supposedly had the power of curing animals with rabies. We didn't have rabies; we just needed a place to stay and were weighing our options when a woman approached and asked if we needed a room. I remember how she just appeared out of nowhere; the thought went through my mind that maybe she was an angel. She said she had a house with several rooms that she rented out. The price was right so we immediately agreed and followed her to the house about three minutes away. Her husband was sitting at the dining room table ready to check us in and take our money. They had a system going; she did the marketing and he was the accountant. We had a very nice small room and bath.

We showered and got settled and went out to eat, finding a *taverna* with a *menú del dia* (menu of the day). We had an *ensalada mixta* (mixed salad of lettuce, tomatoes, shredded carrots, shredded beets, onions, corn, tuna, and a simple vinaigrette.) This was served with a basket of hearty bread and then a second course of delicious meatballs and french fries. It was close to 3:00 and I was ravenously hungry. It had been too long since our croissant and coffee. This all-inclusive *menú del dia* included wine and dessert for only ten euros and I devoured it all. I realized how tired I was, having gotten very little sleep at the big *albergue* in Roncesvalles so after shopping briefly for a phone charger and being told we would have to wait until Pamplona, we went back to our room and rested. I slept. Around 8:00 we realized that though we really weren't hungry we probably would be in the middle of the night, and because we also needed to get up and move so that we actually could sleep that night, we went out again and got a light supper. I had a plate of delicious white asparagus—a regional specialty.

Zubirí to Pamplona

I felt a little tired the next morning. (Surprise!) We hiked mostly on a dirt trail through some woods, and I was dragging even though I was enjoying myself. Around 10:00 I realized my left heel was hurting. I stopped, pulled off my shoe and sock, and saw to my horror that a red blister the size of a nickel had bubbled up on the inside of my heel. A blister? I hike all the time in the Rocky Mountains and I never get blisters! I dug a needle out of my pack and drained the thing and then covered it with a Compeed. I'd read about Compeed in my Camino research and had found some at Walgreens at home though I'd never heard of it before. It's an adhesive patch, a second skin that is supposed to heal up blisters. In the pharmacies along the Camino there was always a huge display of Compeed of many different sizes and shapes; it's a very popular item. (I visited several pharmacies along the Camino; most of my Camino shopping was done in *farmacias*!) I put my sock and shoe back on and we continued our walk. It hurt, not unbearably, but I was aware of it. I was also aware of a stone of fear that had lodged in my heart. Really? A blister? I had been so afraid of getting blisters. The morning we left I told our church family that supposedly only one in a thousand on the Camino doesn't get blisters, and I asked them to pray that I'd be the one! And now, so early! What if it kept me from finishing? This stone of fear was dislodging some of the happiness and delight I'd been feeling. I tried not to let it bother me, but the fear wouldn't go away. And I was so tired today!

Less than an hour later I noticed my other foot was hurting too. I was sure it was my overactive imagination, but the wise thing to do was to check it and, sure enough, there was a matching blister on my right foot. This was very demoralizing. I had to perform the same routine—needle drain, Compeed. I was whining a little to God, a silent "Why, oh why, oh why?" God didn't answer, as the obvious answer was that three days of walking with a heavy pack had taken its toll. A few weeks later when the blisters were healed I realized that maybe it had been for the best that I faced my fears so early in the trip. Maybe God answered my prayers, not with what I asked for, but with what I needed. He gave me a chance to face my fears. Blisters can be bad, but they can be treated, and you can go on.

That stone of fear in my heart was there, but I was determined to live in the moment, to accept what is, to deal with it, and trust God. The next moment is not here yet, so don't live like it is. "Don't assume the worst" was the sermon I preached silently to myself. I thought about the line in the Serenity Prayer— "accepting hardship as a pathway to peace."

We came upon a little café with picnic tables outside filled with *peregrinos* and decided to have lunch. We visited with a couple from Ireland we had met the night before and shared a sandwich. It was good to eat early and the 11:00 *bocadillo* break became our entrenched habit.

There was a bit of confusion leaving the café—conflicting *flechas*. Were we to continue on the road we had just crossed or go up this very steep hill? Someone walking by said that the road was an alternate route—Brian said, "You choose," and I chose, inexplicably, to walk up the steep hill. And I was so glad we did! At the top was a church, the *Iglesia de San Esteban*. It was a little country church all alone on a hill, with a cemetery attached, and a beautiful front yard with big oak trees providing a shady place to sit. "Come in, she said, I'll give you shelter from the storm" was the Bob Dylan line that came to mind, the church being the welcoming woman with her arms stretched wide.

It wasn't an impressive church, but it made a big impression on me. It wasn't the architecture, but yes, prophetically, it was the woman inside with the huge smile and welcoming eyes. She was an old woman, probably in her eighties, who reminded me so much of my beloved Sister Micaela, the Benedictine nun at home. I assume she was a fixture at this church, that she loved the church and she loved the Camino pilgrims who came through and it was her ministry to make them feel welcome and sense the presence of God. She was doing that ministry very well. She didn't speak any English but she quickly determined that was our language and provided a laminated explanation of the church in English. It also had the *Our Father for the Camino* printed on it which I loved, and I expressed that to her as I took a picture of it so I could keep it.

> *Our Father, who is on our way,*
> *May your breath come into us,*
> *And watch over us pilgrims.*
> *Your will be done, in the heat as well as in the cold.*
> *Assist us in our weakness, as we assist those who falter in the way*
> *Lead us not into heartbreak, and deliver us from evil,*
> *In the name of the Father, the Son, and the Holy Spirit.*
> *Amen.*

I gave the woman a hug as I left. I counted this church as a special blessing for the day and the woman as another Camino angel. She communicated love and care through her enthusiasm and smile even though we didn't speak the same language. I was to find many other Camino angels in the days to come.

We kept walking up and down hills on a deserted road and then again into a wooded area. I was dragging again and then realized I hadn't had coffee! I always have coffee at home after lunch. I began to muse and dream of the iced coffee I would have when we got to Pamplona, that is, if we ever got to Pamplona. It sure was taking a long time. We were still in the woods. My feet hurt. Then I realized I hadn't seen iced coffee anywhere and that it might be impossible to get. What would I do? I decided I wanted a Coke. I don't drink Coke too often at home, but it was something caffeinated, and it started sounding so good. Yes, I would get a Coke just as soon as I could. Five minutes later, we came upon a man there in the woods selling cold cans of Coke. This was not a desert mirage, a figment of my imagination. This was real.

I was astonished and thrilled! I was elated! I had heard that the Camino will provide what you need, and this was amazing. It was not really the Coke that I needed but encouragement from God, and that is what I got. We bought a Coke from the man who was also selling candy bars and a few other things. He proudly told us, (in pretty good English!) "I built this place myself." He'd hauled in some rocks to sit on and had carved out a little business, a way to make some money, selling refreshments to *peregrinos* in the woods. He was very outgoing and wanted to chat and we enjoyed sitting on a couple of the rocks and visiting with him while we drank the Coke. I was thankful for him and prayed he'd be blessed and able to support himself. The economic crisis hit Spain hard— unemployment continues to be high.

As we left I asked him how much farther it was to Pamplona and he answered, "Three kilometers." What? I thought we were almost there. Very soon we could see the city but yes, it was still three kilometers before we reached the old city, our destination. My feet were really hurting, and it wasn't the blisters. I felt like I was walking on bruises. Every step hurt. We were soon on flat sidewalk, walking through the modern suburbs of Pamplona. We walked through a downtown business area, blocks and blocks of shops and businesses, all closed for siesta. A majority of the businesses are closed from 2:00 to 4:30 in Northern Spain. I think it's a wonderful idea. People learn to take care of their needs before or after, but siesta is an important cultural value. And everything is closed on Sunday. We talk about the secularization of Western Europe, but in Spain they honor the Sabbath.

Finally, finally, we came around a corner, through a huge park, and saw the wall of the old city. It was impressive—I felt a thrill in seeing it, but we didn't take any time to explore as we had to find someplace to stay. My feet were hurting worse with every step, and my hips! My pack fit me very well and I never had any back or shoulder pain since the weight of the pack was on my hips as it should be. But it sure made them hurt!

We kept walking until we found an *albergue. Complet.* Full. That single word in a hand-lettered sign on the door. Oh dear. We kept walking another five minutes and entered another one. (Brian had an app on his phone that listed the *albergues.* My phone was dead without a charger. Too many pictures!) *Complet.* Full. There was only one more. I was nervous and asked the man at the desk if he knew of any place else we could stay. He said there was a *pensión* we could go to. (A *pensión* is a small, cheap hotel—private rooms but often shared baths.) I asked if he'd call to see if they had a room. He said, "They always do." I asked him if he would mind calling anyway. My feet didn't want to have to take any unnecessary steps. He kindly complied even though he looked busy, told them to expect us, then gave us directions to get there. Those medieval streets are so confusing! We walked, made some wrong turns, came all the way back, and started over. Finally we found the place—a narrow doorway lodged between two other businesses. We opened the door to a long narrow hallway and steps to the second floor. At the top was a friendly Spanish woman with jet black hair who reminded me of a chirping bird— I was surprised she didn't have a flower in her hair! She welcomed us with a smile and walked us into a slightly shabby but perfectly suitable room with two narrow beds covered with chenille bedspreads, a torrent of Spanish flowing from her mouth. When we didn't understand, she just repeated the whole thing, louder, never stopping smiling at us and nodding. Finally we just nodded too. We paid her forty euros and she showed us the community bathrooms down the hall. She finally left us and I collapsed on the bed thanking God as if I'd just checked into a Ritz Carlton.

After a shower, I put on my flipflops and we ventured out. My feet were tender but the change of shoes and the lack of a pack helped immensely. We had walked fifteen miles and I would have loved a rest but we had work to do. The first order of business was to find a phone charger. Brian located an Apple store there in Pamplona; we walked for fifteen minutes to get there and bought one. Second order of business—find a laundromat. That took a lot longer. We walked and walked until we finally found a small one lodged between two restaurants in a big open square. While the wash was running, I charged my dead phone and texted with some friends and family back home. That may have been the day we walked the most miles of the entire Camino.

After our work was done we walked some more, exploring Pamplona, the city of the running of the bulls made famous by the American author Ernest Hemingway. I loved Pamplona. My Enneagram Seven personality daydreamed about coming back here some day and when I realized that I had to remind myself, "You're here now! Don't forget that!" We finally had dinner at 8:30; we had picked a restaurant that didn't open till then and it was worth the wait—an absolutely fabulous meal with a first course of fish soup followed by Iberian pork with mashed potatoes and mashed carrots. Dessert was "French Toast"—listed on the menu just like that even though everything else was in Spanish. It had a resemblance to what I knew as French toast but much better. I was to find a version of this dessert once again in a small café on the other end of the Camino, Villafranca del Bierzo, and it brought back a sweet memory of Pamplona.

We went to bed right after dinner exhausted but happy. I couldn't have been asleep more than five minutes when I was awakened by a noise in the hall, a key fumbling at a lock, and then a low voice in French coming through the thin walls, "*Pardon, madame! Pardon!*" And then more fumbling and apologizing. I smiled in the dark when I realized some poor man had come into the *pensión* and couldn't remember which was his room, trying his key in more than one door that wasn't his. I had a similar experience in Roncesvalles when I tried to find my bed in the long row of identical cubicles after a trip to the bathroom. I imagined him looking like Mr. Magoo from the cartoon I watched in my childhood. After a few attempts he evidently found his room and got inside. Suddenly our room was flooded with light. What? I looked up and there was an open transom between our room and his, and I heard him mumbling and fumbling as he prepared for bed. With a sigh I got out of bed, crossed to the door, opened and went out, and knocked on his door. He jumped up and answered quickly and I simply pointed to the open transom, which had to be closed from his side. He immediately understood and again said, *"Pardon, madame, pardon!"* as he moved to close it. I tried to give him a warm smile so that he could know I wasn't upset with him. He did look a bit like Mr. Magoo. As I got back in bed I said a prayer for him. It didn't take me more than a minute to get back to sleep. And Brian had generously offered to let us sleep a bit longer in the morning as it had been a long, long day. He's trying to keep us on track, I'm feeling a lot more chill.

Pamplona to Meruzabal

t was raining in the morning when we left, just a gentle drizzle. We missed a turn coming out of the city, and immediately a man in a car driving by began to honk and wave, pointing in the opposite direction. We fully understood his meaning and were thankful for him. This happened multiple times on the Camino—we couldn't go any distance at all off track without someone letting us know! In fact, the few times we meant to go off we were stopped and had to communicate, "No, we meant to do this—we know where the Camino is." But that sense of being cared for is lovely—pilgrims feel honored by the locals, welcome and esteemed.

It didn't take long then to leave the city behind or for the rain to stop. Soon we were once again on quiet paths and on our way to the *Alto del Perdon*, the Hill of Forgiveness. This is a big hill with more than a thousand feet of elevation gain, with windmills and incredible views. On the way there, as we enjoyed our *bocadillo* break, I read these lines painted (in Spanish) on the café walls. I could make out some of the meaning but not all, so I texted them to my niece who gave me a translation.

May the wind be favorable to you and blow at your back,
May the rain fall softly on your hair and wash away your troubles.
May the sun shine on your cheeks and illuminate your smile,
May God hold you in the palm of his hand until we return to see
each other.

I received that blessing praying to finish the Camino and finish well. I was a little worried about my feet. The blisters were under control, but my bones ached with every step. When we went back outside, we had to again put on raingear—coats and pack covers. A Chinese man was struggling with a rain poncho and asked if I could help, which I gladly did. He had a huge pack on his back and one in front too! His poncho would barely stretch over all that bulk. "That's an enormous load you're carrying there!" I said. He replied very seriously, "I need a lot of stuff." I smiled, trying not to laugh.

On the way up the steep path under a pleasant sprinkle, I picked wild raspberries alongside the trail and marveled at their sweetness. I visited with a Swedish woman who had four kids at home, ages five to twelve. When I expressed surprise that she was there she said, "My husband can handle everything just fine; I have to walk the Camino." I also talked to some Irish people who always seemed to have a keen sense of humor. They wanted to talk about the American presidential campaign going on at home. One of the men said America should pass a law requiring potential candidates to walk the Camino de Santiago before they can begin their campaigns. We had a laugh together imagining America's presidential candidates sleeping in those *albergue* bunkbeds!

Finally we reached the *Alto del Perdon*, a frequently photographed Camino site "where the path of the wind crosses that of the stars." It's a gorgeous place, but I didn't stay long as my feet hurt so badly. I knew there was another steep hill to climb down, and I knew Brian would quickly catch up. Our goal for the day was the village of Obanos, but after over twelve miles we came across a new *albergue* not listed in our three-year-old guidebook. (Yes, I bought it early, we've been planning this a long time! And I didn't know there was a newer one available!) So I prevailed upon Brian to stop there. He was reluctant, but I can be persuasive, and it turned out to be a very nice place where once again we scored a private room. We had a good meal where we sat by Alaskans and Swedes. German Train Girl was also there, as well as the Chinese man with the two huge packs. He was using his full-size laptop computer that easily weighed ten pounds. We would next see him a couple of weeks later with a tiny daypack. It seems he'd discovered the express delivery services that would take your pack each morning to where you intended to stop for the night for a small fee—lots of people used them every day.

Meruzabal to Villatuerta

The newness of the Camino was wearing off but not the wonder. I was still so full of gratitude, living and enjoying each moment despite the pain in my feet. I was experiencing the Camino as a thin place, a place where the barrier between heaven and earth was thin, a place where the presence of God seemed very close. I saw walking as a work I'd been called to—I felt a sense of purpose and calling in walking. When my feet hurt and I longed to be off them I reminded myself that this was my job and that I'd be finished by early afternoon. I felt a need to walk, to be on the Camino every day. I felt drawn to it, a magnetic pull. What made it such a thin place? I knew it was related to the millions of pilgrims who had walked this way for a thousand years—half a million each year in the twelfth century alone! These people did so because of a desire to know God, to please God, to be blessed by God. They had worn a spiritual path as their feet had worn a physical path. I thought about the "communion of saints" described in the Apostles' Creed, a creed they too had known. I am joined to them somehow; we are all part of that communion in a mysterious unfathomable way.

These early pilgrims walked to Santiago because they believed the remains of St. James were there. These medieval believers wanted to be close to holy people, even dead holy people, and so the veneration of relics became widespread. The origin of the Santiago phenomenon is a story told in many ways—here is one version.

Santiago (St. James) was said to have left Jerusalem and gone to the "ends of the earth" to preach the good news of Jesus Christ. He later returned to Jerusalem where the Book of Acts tells us he was martyred. His body was put onto a magical ship that floated up on the shores of the Iberian Peninsula at a place called Finisterre, which literally means "end of the earth." He was buried, but his grave was hidden as protection from looting and somehow became lost for eight hundred years, at which time his remains were mysteriously found; he was then entombed in Compostella, the Field of Stars, after a shepherd saw a sign in the sky. Pilgrims began to flock to the church that was built there seeking miracles, forgiveness, and answers to prayers. And thus the Camino was born.

We'd had *tostadas* and *café con leche* again for breakfast. I had to work to remember that *tostadas* were not what I thought of as tostadas but actually just toast. I kept wanting to order "tosta," which is…nothing? And a *tortilla* wasn't a tortilla—it was a potato omelet.

Brian liked them, but I preferred *tostadas*. That is, toast. With *mermelada*. Marmelade. Jam. Jelly. I remember being about seven years old and realizing that what our family called a couch, other people called a sofa. And my grandmother called a divan! A divan! Such an exotic word for a couch. She had a divan—we just had a couch.

I was looking forward to our 11:00 *bocadillo* break. We were hungry by then after walking three or four hours on toast alone. But it was Sunday, and when we walked through the village we had planned to eat in there was absolutely nothing open. I remembered that I'd thrown out some leftover bread that morning and Brian said he'd thrown out some cheese; we ended up sharing a fruit rollup and a Kind bar. We walked another hour, however, and were happy to find a *bocadillo* and fresh-squeezed orange juice, or *zumo de naranja*, which in Mexico is called *jugo de naranja*. Language. It's fascinating but confusing!

We walked fourteen miles that day and I was desperate for some relief from the foot pain. It just felt like I was walking on bruises—every single step hurt. When I took my shoes off at the *albergue* as we were checking in to leave them in the reception area as required, I could hardly walk on the hard stone floor. I recalled while walking that day that I'd once had similar foot pain, hiking in the Rocky Mountains with a particular pair of boots, and how new insoles had made a huge difference. I asked the American woman working there if she knew where I could buy some. She said we were in luck—there was a large sporting goods store only an hour's walk ahead, right on the Camino. But it didn't open till 10:00 tomorrow and we would arrive much earlier if we left at our regular time. I was quite resourceful, though, and suggested a great way to avoid that—we could sleep in, getting up at 7:30 instead of 6:00! As far as being "in luck," I once again marveled that the Camino seemed to be a place where whatever it is you

really need is provided. (If we had been a day ahead and arrived
there Sunday it wouldn't have been open at all!) Brian readily
agreed even though he was quick to point out we would not make
the miles we had planned for that day. I kept reminding him we
had plenty of time, that the reason we had planned seven weeks
away instead of six was so that we wouldn't feel any time
pressures. It is hard for him not to be driven. But I appreciate that
the drive and determination he has is mostly a positive force in his
life and so I'm not complaining!

The building the *albergue* occupied was over four hundred
years old; it was fabulous. We were in a room on the third floor.
Everything was stone, and the stone floor in our room had a huge
dip in the middle, but I figured it had been standing for four
hundred years and wasn't likely to collapse any time soon. The
ceiling was made of crooked wooden beams and plaster.

We had dinner that night at the *albergue* with Patsy and Andrew,
devoted Catholics from South Africa, and had great conversation
about life, the Camino, church, and the world we live in. Marcia and
Charlie, the Alaskans we'd met a few nights ago, were also there,
along with another guy from Canada. We threw our small laundry
loads in together and sat and visited while we waited.

Villatuerta to Villamayor de Monjardin

I t was a treat to sleep in. We walked an hour into Estella where we found a café serving breakfast *bocadillos*, slightly different than a standard *bocadillo*—they were smaller and the bread was softer. It was a nice change and we leisurely had a couple of coffees before going off to find Decathalon, the big sporting goods store. I was thrilled to find and buy some Ironman gel insoles and they eased the pain a little. Shortly after we left the city of Estella we encountered…a wine fountain! For real! Yes, the Bodegas Irache, a historic winery started by Benedictine monks, has installed a fountain that pilgrims can draw wine from. It's such a surprise! And just past the wine fountain was a blacksmith who was hard at work over his forge, pounding out his wares. We each bought a small iron scallop shell that he attached to the front of our packs. He then gave us fruit from a tree right next to where he was working. I didn't recognize this fruit and he had to show us how to break them open to eat. It was pink and delicious and tasted a little like kiwi. Again, this man had such a kind and welcoming spirit that opened up our spirits and left us feeling joyful and refreshed.

We walked only nine miles that day and stopped at the little town of Villamayor de Monjardin. We found a nice *albergue* and

were third in line to check in behind a group of five women and
another couple. The women got a room with five beds and were
happy about that. The couple asked for a private room and I was
surprised that another one was available when they got to us. This
albergue was run by a Dutch Christian ministry, and their
building too was over four hundred years old.

There was a tiny bar next to the *albergue*, probably the only
place to eat in Villamayor, and we sat down at one of the few
tables. The waitress came immediately to take our order with pad
and pencil in hand. I said, "Uh, la menu?" Yes, I was asking to see
a menu—she said *"Sí,"* quickly turned and then came back with
placemats and settings. Somehow I understood what had
happened; we had just ordered "the menu." The *menú del dia*.
And I realized that was just fine; we were hungry! She then gave
us our choices and the only thing I understood was *sopa* and
ensalada. So I had an awesome green salad with white asparagus
and Brian had a seafood soup he raved over. That was the first
course. I then had *pescado* while he had *pollo* (fish and chicken).
Do I feel badly that most of the Spanish I learned while on the
Camino was related to eating? No, I do not. We also had rosé
wine, flan for dessert, and coffee. All for eleven euros each—
simply amazing. Yes, wine is ubiquitous in Spanish culture. We
would soon be walking through one of the premier wine-
producing regions in the world, La Rioja. Wine is an accepted
part of every good meal. Most people drink wine every day. I
never saw any obvious abuse or drunkenness. They just seem to
enjoy it!

We visited the village church in the afternoon. The door was
unlocked but it was dark inside. You can, however, put a euro in a
machine and the lights go on for about a minute. It was like the
shower in our *albergue* where you have to keep pushing a button
to keep the water flowing. The shower at this *albergue*, a tiny box

oddly stuck in the corner of the main stairway, required six or eight pushes for what I considered a very short shower. This was not nearly as bothersome as some of the motion-activated lights we encountered in Spain almost everywhere. In many restrooms you must stay in constant motion in order for the lights to continue to burn. This can be a little funny at times, requiring you to wave your hands over your head while sitting. Walking down hotel corridors, lights in front of you snap on as others behind you snap off. All good energy saving measures, I'm sure, but there was frequently a delay in the lights flickering back on which resulted in some moments that were both frantic and comical. More than once I caught myself mumbling "Good grief!" under my breath.

Our room at the *albergue* was charming—tiny and spartan, but the bed was nicely made and adorned with a spray of plastic roses and a couple of pretty floral pillows. It sounds a bit cheesy but it was noticed and appreciated. There was a small leaded glass window and the view was priceless. We also spent some afternoon time sitting out in front of the *albergue* on a terrace that looked down on the Camino below. They had put out some plastic chairs and there was a bit of shade from the building itself. Pilgrims were visiting together, reading, writing in journals. People continued to arrive throughout the afternoon and the *hospitaleros* would register them right there at a picnic table. Most of the rooms at this *albergue* were small—probably the largest would accommodate no more than eight people. It was laid out in a sort of hodge-podge way, like the shower we used in the corner of the stairway, and some people had to walk through other people's sleeping quarters to get to the restrooms but this did nothing to detract from the overall charming atmosphere.

And then finally the *hospitalero* closed up shop and put out a large sign that said, "*Complet.*" I knew what that meant. An hour later I watched a single man wearily climb the steps to the terrace and ask if there was any space. He was offered a mattress which could be put in a spot on the basement floor. "But there are two of us," he said. I appreciated the *hospitalero's* efforts as he said, "You are welcome to share it." The pilgrim declined and went on. I have no idea where they slept that night.

We all gathered in the dining room at 7:00 for dinner, sitting at picnic tables which were probably custom-made to take advantage of every bit of space in the dining room. Our host offered thanks to God for the meal, something which hadn't been done before and which I greatly appreciated. Dinner was salad with feta cheese and shepherd's pie. I smiled when it was served, remembering how on my first trip to India after a week of very spicy Indian food we took a side trip to Darjeeling, high in the Himalayas, and stayed in a hostel that had once upon a time been the home of a British tea plantation owner. I almost wept with joy at dinner when shepherd's pie, an iconic British dish, the ultimate comfort food, was served.

This shepherd's pie was delicious, very different from those I've had before. I wish I had the recipe for it so I could make it at home. We had pudding for dessert and then the host got up to speak very briefly. He offered little booklets of the Gospel of John in several different languages. It was a gracious gift, given in a gracious way, and I think everyone there took one. He then invited us all to a "Jesus Meditation Service" that would take place at 8:00. Of course Brian and I were eager to attend, unsure if there would be many others.

We arrived shortly beforehand to a room set slightly apart from the main *albergue*, part of the same building but with a separate entrance. We walked into a candlelit room with pillows lining all the walls. We all sat on the floor in our own very comfortable spaces and waited quietly for the "Jesus Meditation

Service" to begin. It was such a peaceful atmosphere. The pilgrims came in one by one and found seats, and shortly before the service began a final lone pilgrim entered and claimed the last available seat. It seemed just right.

We sat quietly for the next hour listening to soft and gentle music. Within that hour three passages of Scripture were read, each in three languages—Spanish, English, and German. One of the passages was the very familiar quotation from Jesus, *"Come to me, all you who are weary and heavy laden, and I will give you rest."*

As I listened to that invitation from Jesus that night, I heard it differently than ever before. We were all pilgrims on the Camino, on a journey with a destination in mind. We carried our burdens, our packs, and they were all different, but they were heavy. We were all weary. What had happened to us that day? We had been invited into a place of rest, a place to stop and lay down our burdens for a while. We had each been given a bed, a promise of a night's sleep. We had been well fed, and good food is such a comfort. Any food will give you calories which convert to physical energy, but delicious food gives you a sense of contentment and well-being—good food also nourishes the soul.

But it was never intended that we move permanently into this *albergue*! If the next morning we'd said, "It's been so nice here, we're going to stay," we would have been kindly told that was impossible. The purpose of the *albergue* is not to take people permanently off the Camino, off the Way, but to give them what they need to stay on it!

How many times had I begged Jesus to take my burdens away permanently? How many times had I listened to that scripture and thought to myself that it didn't "work," at least not for me. I still felt burdened. I still had things in my life I didn't like, problems I didn't want to carry, difficulties I wanted to escape.

That night I heard those words of Jesus anew. I finally got it.

Jesus doesn't want me to escape. Jesus invites me to keep living and not give up. He cares for me, nourishes me, and provides what I need. But he does so that I might grow up into the fullness of who I was created to be—to work together with him to right what is wrong in the world. To be a co-laborer in his creation. To participate in restoring all things unto himself. To be a part of finishing what he'd begun. To face the challenges of life with faith, hope, and love, not to escape them. This was a profound paradigm shift for me and I went to bed full of wonder, ready to get back on the trail in the morning.

Villamayor de Monjardín to Torres del Río

I was awake often throughout the night but felt such a sense of peace and joy that I was glad I wasn't missing out by being asleep. I just couldn't stop smiling. Exactly the kind of problem I like having! We had set the alarm for 6:30, but we were up at 6:15 and on the road by 6:45 with our headlamps. Our kind *hospitalero* had been good to us but he wasn't exactly God

Almighty, able to meet all our needs; he too was subject to human limitations and had announced with regret at dinner that due to being short-staffed there would be no breakfast in the morning. We hiked half an hour until we were able to turn off headlamps and made good time—eight and a half miles in three hours all the way to Los Arcos where we could finally get some breakfast. Along the way we had passed another concession trailer like the one up in the mountains but they were just starting to set up for the lunch crowd and had nothing to offer us.

Early mornings the sun was always behind us and we cast long shadows on the road ahead. Memories of those shadows, the warm sun, the beautiful countryside, and the dirt roads we walked down are vibrant memories that warm my heart even now. That morning we walked and chatted a bit with a young French woman who grew up in Normandy and now lived in Calgary, Canada. She spoke perfect English—I told her I had studied French in high school but had very little opportunity to use it so she began to talk to me in French. She was very patient and allowed me to fumble along. She told me she was hiking alone, that she'd left a boyfriend in Canada and didn't want to be away from him too long so she was hiking very long days in an attempt to finish. She had only a certain number of days till she needed to return to Canada and wanted to spend some time with her parents in Normandy, too. She soon bid her "*au revoir, buen camino*" and left us in the dust.

Los Arcos was a good-sized town with lots to see but not enough time to see it. I was so grateful we had more time than most but I frequently cast longing looks back as we passed beautiful buildings or places I wanted to explore. I loved sitting in the towns and watching people—*peregrinos* and locals alike. We sat near a fountain in a small plaza outside a beautiful church and enjoyed a chocolate croissant, *café con leche,* and orange juice. I took off my shoes and socks and soothed my burning feet on the smooth cool pavement. Yes, they were better with the new insoles but far from pain-free. And yet I was able to trust and be at peace with my feet. I was practicing living in the moment, not worrying about the future, trusting God's grace to continue to carry me forward. It felt so good to do that, to surrender myself to that grace, to cease striving and to know that he is God.

We passed through so many beautiful vineyards that day, row after row of vines heavily laden with big healthy beautiful grapes ready for harvest soon. The vineyards were impeccably tended and pruned with not a weed in sight. They spoke to me of the overflowing abundance and lovingkindness of God. We came upon a herd of sheep being led from one pasture to another. Brian had got ahead of me a hundred yards or so as I got distracted by something (which happened often), and the sheep came onto the road between us and kept us separated for a while. I couldn't stop grinning and I can't stop grinning now as I remember it.

We entered the town of Torres del Rio, found an *albergue* quickly, and used the washing machine to launder all our clothes. I chatted online with my friend Anne-Marie in South Africa. She knew my feet were still hurting and asked me to send a picture so she could lay her hands on my "virtual" feet and pray. Of course I immediately did so—I'll take all the prayer I can get. My pinky toe was red and hot and inflamed in addition to the feeling of walking on bruises. (The nail eventually fell off!) She typed me her prayer and as I started to read it I thought to myself, "Don't just read that prayer, breathe it in!" as if she was really here with me praying for my feet. I closed my eyes and did so—no fanfare, just a moment of faith. We hung the clothes out to dry and went to find some lunch. It was now mid-afternoon, but we'd had a late breakfast. We found a nice place and had a salad and *pollo con biere*, a regional specialty, which was delicious and very filling. We went back to the room and slept the rest of the afternoon away.

Lying awake enjoying the presence of God the night before had caught up with me.

There was a church in Torres del Rio that is somewhat famous, known as the Little Holy Sepulchre after the church in Jerusalem—it also is an octagonal church. We wanted to see the church and had found it locked before we went to lunch, a sign indicating it would be open from 4:00 to 7:00. After our naps we went back but found it still locked. There was a phone number posted on the sign if you wanted to see it after hours. I went to the bar next door and asked the bartender about it—he immediately made a call and when I walked back a woman was hustling down the street with keys in hand. She opened up the church (forty-five minutes late) and we and a few others who had gathered went inside.

It was a tiny church hardly bigger than a big living room, a stone bench along the walls to sit on and some standing room in the center. I smiled to think of the comparison with the mammoth Holy Sepulchre Church in Jerusalem, one of the most significant churches in the world. But the presence of God was in that place. A medieval crucifix particularly spoke to me and to Brian too.

That night our *albergue* was serving pilgrim meals in the *comedor*, but we weren't very hungry. There was a large menu of *raciones* (small plates of snack food) posted outside on the patio. We picked three—Iberian ham, fried calamari, and cheese croquettes, and went into the bar, sat down, and ordered. The bartender pulled out his cell phone, made a call, and apparently sent our order on. It wasn't long before we were served more food than we could eat.

On the other side of a partition sat all the *peregrinos* in the *comedor* eating their *menú del dias*. An American man we had met in Pamplona was there who was hiking the Camino with his eleven-year-old son. He had told us he'd done it a few years before by himself and had wanted to take his son someday when he was older. With all the political instability our world has experienced recently he worried that the Camino could become unsafe and decided to take him now. The boy seemed to be having a good time and we would encounter them a couple more times down the road. The father came over to our table to say hello and then, pointing to our plates, "Where'd you get that?" He was a bit jealous. When we'd eaten all we wanted and were ready to head back to our room I took them a plate of leftovers.

Back in the room we watched an old American western from the 1960s with Spanish overdubbing. It was ridiculously funny— the overplayed parts, the absurd good guy/bad guy stereotypes. Oh that our world can someday see beyond this and move beyond!

Torres del Río to Logroño

I slept more than nine hours, but when the alarm went off at 7:00 my first thought was, "I can't do this again!" I got up anyway and we were on the Camino by 7:45 after coffee at the corner café. Amazingly, once we were on the road I felt strong and energetic and we walked over seven miles to Viana by 10:15. There we had a second, more substantial breakfast. We bought some gel insoles for Brian, whose feet were hurting increasingly worse even as mine were getting better.

We passed an old man harvesting something off his trees right alongside the dirt path we were walking—harvesting the same way I'd seen the olive harvest gathered in Israel—big tarps under the trees covered with huge piles of some kind of fruit. They were bigger than olives, almost the size of small plums, and I asked him "*Qué es esto?*" The problem with knowing a few Spanish phrases is not in being understood, it's the responses you get back that also come in Spanish, and you have no idea what's been said. The man was very friendly, repeated himself a couple of times, and then gave me a handful. Only when I examined them did I realize what he'd said—"*Almondas.*" Almonds. Of course. And delicious right off the tree!

We continued the trek into Logroño and came upon two priests in long black robes greeting pilgrims as they passed by. They spoke a little English and I asked them what kind of priests they were— Benedictine, Franciscan? No, they were emphatic they didn't belong to any order but were a community of priests living together in order to minister to needy people; they mentioned working to get prostitutes off the streets and living better lives. One of the priests was working on a wood carving, a large flat piece of wood in his lap; it was an impressive piece of work which he described as an icon which he would later paint. I said a silent prayer for them as we walked on, entering the outskirts of Logroño, walking a long way through industrial areas. Finally we crossed a big river, the Ebro, on a magnificent ancient bridge and entered into the heart of the city. We had also just entered into La Rioja, the world-famous wine-producing province of Spain.

Crossing the bridge, we immediately encountered huge crowds and learned we'd arrived in Logroño for the annual *Fiesta San Mateo*, or Feast of St. Matthew, which has become a celebration of the grape harvest. There were food booths, crafts, lots of people dressed in traditional costumes, big stages set up with live music. We walked nearly a kilometer to find the *pensión* where we had a reservation; the festival and crowds stretched on for the entire way.

Our phone GPS led us to the address in the downtown area. There was no sign, just a note on the mailbox which said the *pensión* was on the second floor. We rang the bell and a buzzer sounded as someone let us in. We climbed to the second floor and found a hallway of doors; one said "*Pensión*" and had a smiley face door knocker that said "*Jesús te ama*." (Jesus loves you!) The young woman running the *pensión* showed us to a tiny but clean room with a bathroom down the hall. We took showers and then a very short nap.

We went for a late lunch at a crowded restaurant, the "Drunken Duck," and ordered the *menú del dia*. First course was a delicious salad with some sort of warm black and white noodles on top; they were especially tasty and I later found out these "noodles" were baby squid. Then a tuna steak with tomato sauce followed by flan for dessert. After lunch we enjoyed the fiesta. Supposedly there was a demonstration of grape stomping somewhere but we never found it. It was enough just to wander in the city and watch the people— families with children and strollers, happy people enjoying life. I paid a street artist to paint a temporary Camino tattoo on my arm. It was a beautiful, sunshiny, perfect day.

In the evening we attended mass at the cathedral, a special mass because of the feast day. The church was full and it was good to take communion. Afterwards we walked some more, got some tapas, and then back to the room to go to bed. *Peregrinos* shouldn't stay up late although I later talked to some who did and ended up staying an extra day in Logroño. We enjoyed Logroño and were happy to have been there for the fiesta, but we were up early and ready to go in the morning.

Logroño to Ventosa

I always enjoyed being out walking before dawn in the early morning darkness. There is an excitement about being up before the rest of the world and that's not a hard thing to do in Spain, the latest of the late night cultures. Many restaurants don't open till 8:30 or 9:00, but fortunately those who cater to the Camino crowd know that pilgrims operate on a different schedule. Still it's common to be unable to get an evening meal before 7:00.

Therefore the only places open in the early morning hours are the cafes serving pilgrims, little welcoming oases of light in otherwise dark neighborhoods. Many of the *albergues* would serve toast and coffee, and many of the *pensións* and Camino hotels had cafés. If not, we'd walk until we found one, usually just a few minutes.

It was beginning to be light as we made it through the outskirts of Logroño. We walked past a big lake and came upon a man in a booth with long white hair and a long white beard selling candy, Camino pins, and walking sticks he'd made. He does this out of love and care for the *peregrinos* and also stamps their *credenciales*. All the stamps are different, custom-designed for each place offering stamps. His was of a donkey, reminding me of the peace-preaching Jesus making his triumphant entry into Jerusalem. The man had also trained a squirrel to come to him when he called; could he be a modern-day St. Francis? The moment he stamped my *credencial*, the memory of a dream I'd had in the night came as a flash. I'd dreamed of a woman stamping my *credencial* and writing, "The way of mercy leads to justice." It seemed significant and I spent much of the morning pondering this. I want to walk the world as the mercy of God. I'm walking the Camino de Santiago now, and I know that it's a preparation for the rest of my life. I want the mercy I show to others to lead to justice and I know it can, but sometimes what I can do seems so small and insignificant. Lord, make me an instrument of your peace, a conduit of your mercy!

The morning walk was peaceful and easy. The vineyards were achingly beautiful. We had our *bocadillo* break in Nájera and visited the church there. But the sun came out in force afterwards; it was hot, there was little shade, and Brian's blisters were worse. We were moving slowly and had five miles left to get to Ventosa where we thankfully had a reservation. We found the hotel which was very small, just six rooms; a sign on the door said "*Complet*" which made me more grateful for that reservation. We rang the bell and a very elegant Spanish woman greeted us.

The hotel seemed like a home, an elegant home that fit this elegant woman, furnished with antiques and classic tapestries. We entered into the living room which had an out-of-place shoe rack along one wall—a concession to the clientele. She asked us to take off our shoes and leave them and our walking poles there. While we were doing that she said that there had been a cancellation and for five euros more we could have the best room in the house. Well, of course! Five euros almost seemed like a joke.

After stamping our *credenciales* she told us that she offered a communal dinner each evening for those guests who wanted to participate. We readily agreed and she showed us to our room, the best one in the house! The room was small but very classy. The bathroom was extra nice. I was so impressed by the big fluffy towels. I don't really know if they were so very special or just in contrast to the well-used and faded ones I'd been using in *albergues* or, when none were provided, the very thin "quick-dry" synthetic camping towel we each carried in our packs. I took a shower and then savored the luxuriousness of those towels. Our spartan lifestyle was creating a gratitude in me for extra nice things when we experienced them.

I then took down all our dirty laundry, pretty much everything we had. Our hostess had offered to do it but I was a little embarrassed to hand it over to this chic, sophisticated woman. I said, "I can do it, just show me the machine!" She responded, "This is a hotel! I will not let you do the laundry!" So I handed it over and it came back an hour and a half later very neatly folded, smelling much better than it had such a short time earlier. Oh, the marvel of modern washing machines and dryers— they never cease to amaze me.

The home was truly beautiful. She told us she and her husband had bought it a few years before and did extensive renovations to turn it into this lovely hotel. It was an eighteenth-century building now on a historic registry that had been subdivided into apartments and had been a labor of love for them to remodel. There was an exquisite library sitting room on the second floor with lots of windows and I sat for an hour in the afternoon reading after examining the titles on the shelf, many in English. I later complimented her on her tastes in books and she told me those were just her "public" books, ones she wouldn't mind too much losing if someone were to walk away with one. She said she has a lot more at home, her favorites, which she really wouldn't want to lose. I very much empathize with that—my books are precious to me, and yes, I tend to hoard them and protect them. She said she works very hard during the Camino season but then takes several winter months off during which time she reads voluminously. This year she will also visit her son who lives in Santiago. Not in Santiago, Spain, but ironically, Santiago, Chile!

Around 5:00 our hostess called our room to tell us that all the other guests had opted out of dinner, were going out for pizza, but that she'd be happy to cook for us alone if we wanted. I initially protested, saying I didn't want her to go to the trouble just for the two of us, but again she said, "This is a hotel, this is what I do—I'd love to cook for you." And so again I dutifully acquiesced and sat for a bit in the beautiful garden, being for a few hours not a Camino walker but very much a lady of leisure.

We came down to dinner at 7:00 as requested and walked into a dining room with a long table intended for a crowd but set just for two, with beautiful china and crystal and linen napkins, as for a king and queen. It was exquisite. Dinner was a beautiful green salad with tomato, corn, shredded beets and carrots, oranges, apples and a nice balsamic dressing. The main course was a skillet of chicken paella with roasted red peppers—cooked perfectly. Again, I am reminded of Jesus inviting us in off the Camino, satisfying our every need and desire, and then sending us out in the morning, refreshed and ready to go. I slept nine blissful, peaceful hours that night.

Ventosa to Azofra

We met some of the other guests at breakfast—five American women walking together, probably in their sixties. Two of them have lived in Barcelona for forty years and the others are old friends who still live in the United States. They explained that one of them had taken a taxi to be here, was taking a taxi back to where she'd left off, one was staying another day before taking a taxi to meet the group elsewhere—it all sounded complicated and stressful. I'm glad we are just walking, no taxis, no baggage service. I'm not judging their Camino, just grateful for mine. They were friendly and one gave me her phone number in case we need anything when we are in Barcelona after our Camino is finished which was very kind of her.

The first part of our walk that day was very peaceful, lots of quiet time to meditate, to simply be. All we had to do was walk through beautiful vineyards and I loved that. We passed a guitarist with a harmonica singing sweet music on the side of the path just for the pilgrims passing by! I stopped, closed my eyes, and breathed in the music, and Brian put some coins in his hat.

My feet were much better. The blisters were healing nicely, although still covered in Compeed, and overall they just weren't aching like they had. I had sensed a difference the day after Anne-Marie had "type-prayed" and I had breathed that prayer in, in faith. Something else to feel grateful for and to marvel over. Prayer is such a mystery—I don't know how it works, and at the same time I have a sense that I'm not meant to, don't need to, I just need to trust and obey. Thank you, Lord, that my feet aren't hurting, I am so, so grateful. And somehow even grateful that they had hurt so badly, so I could appreciate the goodness of them not hurting.

We did see our "Chinese Friend of the Big Pack," who now had a very small pack, a teeny-tiny pack. He told us his name was Benjamin and explained that he wanted to jog now so had sent it on. I was happy for him. My twenty-pound pack is heavy enough but his was thirty pounds heavier! I was amused hearing him say he wanted to jog. Nobody jogs the Camino. There are no runners. Except for Benjamin. He wasn't jogging when I saw him. I never saw him or anyone else jog. But if a desire to jog allows him to justify not carrying the ridiculously heavy pack, I support him fully. Whatever works. Everyone has to do their own Camino.

We walked into Azofra, another little ghost town that might not exist today were it not for the Camino. The official population is five hundred, but there were almost no people out except some pilgrims sitting in front of an *albergue*. We walked through the town looking for the *pensión* we had booked and finally found it. The door was locked with the familiar "*Complet*" sign out. Brian knocked on the door, a man answered, we explained we had a reservation, and he said, "Well, I can't let you in. I'm just a guest here. You'll have to go ask for Julio down at the bar."

The bar was down the big hill we'd just climbed to get to the *pensión* and Brian took off his pack before going back down while I sat on the stoop and waited. Brian later told me he'd imagined finding Julio drinking at the bar but Julio was in fact running the bar, which was very busy. He stopped long enough to run up the hill to show us to our room and said he'd get us registered later. The room was plain but large and clean with three twin beds and a big balcony. It was too hot to sit on the balcony in the afternoon with sun blazing down on it, but the clothes we washed in the shared bathroom down the hall dried in a hurry out there.

We rested and read in the afternoon and after supper at the bar enjoyed the view from our balcony. The church directly in front of us was old and had an annex which had served as a Camino hostel centuries ago. It wasn't hard to imagine being a medieval pilgrim in Azofra.

Azofra to Santo Domingo de la Calzada

Another early start with headlamps and, much later as I write this, I still remember the sunrise that morning. There wasn't anything particularly noteworthy about it except it was a sunrise, it was beautiful, and I was aware of how spectacularly special every sunrise is if we will only see it for the miracle it is. I thank G.K. Chesterton for this memorable quote which helps me to remember this truth:

"Because children have abounding vitality, because they are in spirit fierce and free, therefore they want things repeated and unchanged. They always say, 'Do it again'; and the grown-up person does it again until he is nearly dead. For grown-up people are not strong enough to exult in monotony. But perhaps God is strong enough to exult in monotony. It is possible that God says every morning, 'Do it again' to the sun; and every evening, 'Do it again' to the moon. It may not be automatic necessity that makes all daisies alike; it may be that God makes every daisy separately, but has never got tired of making them. It may be that He has the eternal appetite of infancy; for we have sinned and grown old, and our Father is younger than we."

Each and every morning that we were walking before dawn we would always turn around and acknowledge the sun when it came peeking up over the horizon, always from behind as we were always walking west. We were blessedly free from the distractions that usually plague us, with nothing to do but walk on the Camino and notice the sunrise. I was walking with three Irish women that morning, two of them friends who'd come to walk the Camino together and one who had just met the others and joined them. They were all Irish but the woman on her own was a Belfast woman from Northern Ireland while the other two were from Dublin, from the Republic. Not a big difference in many American's eyes but it is to someone living there. The Republic is an independent Irish nation, while Northern Ireland is still ruled by the British Crown. Despite centuries of bloody animosity between Irish Catholics and Loyalist Protestants, things have thankfully been mostly peaceful in recent decades. May peace continue there, oh God.

When I told the Belfast woman I'd been to her country just a few months earlier, she wittily said, "You were in Belfast in May and you didn't come to me birthday party?" She also told me she is doing the Camino to "figure out her life." She said she "fights with a lot of people but it's not always my fault." I never figured out if that was a heartfelt admission to the pain in her life or just another Irishman telling a tall tale with a wink and a grin. Maybe a little bit of both.

I stopped walking to take a swig from my water bottle and tie my shoe, and when I started up again I found myself alongside one of the other Irishwomen, one of the Dubliners. When she learned I lived in Missouri, she said her daughter had lived for a while in St. Louis and had had an extended gig with her band playing in a Irish-themed bar there. She wryly told me her daughter came home with an American souvenir, the baby growing in her belly, who is now her beloved and only 9-year-old granddaughter. It's a stereotype, I know, but the Irish I encountered on the Camino were always witty and fun.

Santo Domingo de la Calzada wasn't very far but I had read about it and really wanted to stay there so we made a rather short day of it. It's a historic Camino town named after an early Camino hero, Domingo Garcia, who was born in 1019 and had been thwarted in his desire to serve God by becoming a monk. After being rejected by the local monastery, he dedicated his life to building roads, bridges, and hospitals to care for peregrinos on the Camino. He was declared a saint after his death, Santo Domingo de la Calzada, and there are statues commemorating his life—a case where the great disappointment of his life actually resulted in even greater blessing. What a reminder to me to let go of control and trust that God is at work in my life even when I don't see it.

And the town did not disappoint! There was a lot happening in this little city of six thousand people that still retains its medieval charm—lots of busy restaurants, shops, churches, and museums. It was a delight to walk into the city and imagine how it might have looked eight hundred years ago. We walked to the church and saw that the pilgrim hospital adjacent and originally built by Santo Domingo had been turned into a hotel. We walked in to inquire about a room and were told that it was *"Complet."* At noon! But then the desk clerk told us they had a sister hotel in the city, just a few minutes away, that had previously been a fourteenth-century convent. She offered to call and see if they had any free rooms, and they had one only, so we booked it and got directions to walk there immediately. I wish now I had taken some time to explore the lobby and public areas of this hotel but the one we ended up in was also beautiful—the Parador de Santa Domingo Bernardo de Fresnada. It was a bit of a splurge but we loved it, and honestly, I've paid more for cheap chain hotels at home.

We walked through the busy streets and had a nice leisurely lunch at an outdoor table. Brian had *Iberian jamon* and *calamari*, I had *tortellini a spinaci*. We recognized some familiar *peregrinos* walking by—two Swedish women we'd begun to know and were to come to know better later, Mona and Caren, and later two friendly young British girls walking jauntily by in shorts and flipflops, a real change from when we'd passed them yesterday moving very slowly because of a bad knee. We visited with both pairs. The British girls confessed sheepishly that they'd been there since the day before, having given up and taken a cab. We never saw them after that day.

We walked around admiring the gorgeous city and made plans to go to a Cistercian vesper service at 6:30. I wanted to continue to explore the city but by 4:00 I begrudgingly admitted to myself that I had to have a nap. The Parador was calling my name.

We slept more than an hour and left to go to the church with just a little time to spare. When we arrived we joined other pilgrims waiting to get in, a locked gate keeping us outside. The gate remained locked and the church dark until just a couple of minutes before the service was scheduled to begin. Some people began to wonder aloud if perhaps there would be no service tonight. I told them not to worry, that monastics live by the clock. Right on time, a bell began to toll, an interior door opened, and nuns in traditional long black habits and headdresses began to quickly file in like clockwork—like the figures on an elaborate cuckoo clock. It was almost comical. One flipped on the lights, another came and unlocked the door, and the rest filed into the choir. The congregation filed in far less methodically and found places to sit and watch while they sang their vespers for twenty-five minutes; we then watched them file out the same door they'd come in. It was intermission. A pilgrim blessing service was scheduled for 7:00 and the lead nun came out assisting a very old priest with two canes. She led him to a chair behind the altar table where he read a fifty-minute mass in Spanish. (What was I expecting?) At the end we went forward and received Communion and that made it all worthwhile.

Santo Domingo de la Calzada to Belorado

I t had been a good day in Santo Domingo, but I was so tired. I found myself worrying through the night—how could I be so tired? I'd given up exploring and taken a nap, for Pete's sake! My feet ached even in bed. And today we'd only walked ten miles—tomorrow was going to be a full fifteen! Was I crazy to think I could walk five hundred miles with this big pack? How much more would I suffer?

So I arose early the next morning in the darkness with fear and trepidation. And then went and had a great day! I felt so strong all day long and had such joy. Walking seemed easy and was a delight. Mysterious. I think I learned a little bit more that day not to take my worries so seriously. Not to take myself so seriously. To live even deeper into the moment I have and trust that the next moment will take care of itself. If only I could learn that fully and give up worry altogether! But I'm accepting a little more deeply the fact that we never fully arrive at that place, but live out our faith moment by moment, day by day.

We walked five miles to breakfast in Grañon, walked up to a busy café, and heard a favorite Bob Dylan song playing. *"Sara, Sara, sweet virgin angel, sweet love of my life, Sara, Sara, radiant jewel, mystical wife."* Hearing Bob Dylan tunes makes Brian really happy—it makes me really happy, too! Brian was spending part of each day quoting Dylan lyrics to me—whole songs. Sometimes he'd need to look up the words but he knew many of them in full. It was a fun added dimension to our walks. He sang along with this one all the way through.

There was a small church open across from the café that we visited. It was open but empty. On a Sunday morning! There's a real sadness in that. We visited so many churches and went to every service we could. Many of them were full but we also saw many closed churches, decommissioned churches no longer operating as churches. At the same time there is a river of people moving along the Camino de Santiago hungry for God and for spiritual fulfillment. Lord have mercy!

The Camino took us through several small villages on our way to Belorado. Viloria de Rioja celebrates their patron, the famous Brazilian author Paulo Coehlo, who wrote his first book when he was forty years old, *The Pilgrimage,* about the Camino. He walked the Camino and it forever changed his life. I hadn't read it, but I'd read one of his lesser-known books, *By The River Piedra We Sat Down and Wept,* and had loved it, as well as *The Alchemist.* Paulo Coehlo is now one of the world's best-selling authors.

We made a couple of phone calls along the way to places in Belorado, but everything was *complet.* Brian had become quite adept at making reservations on the phone in Spanish. Usually it worked out, but we didn't have a place entering into Belorado. Right before we got to town, however, a man drove slowly down the road offering free bottles of water to pilgrims with the name of his *albergue* printed on the side—a great way to advertise!

We stopped at the first *albergue* we saw, attracted by a shady, grassy garden where some peregrinos were relaxing, and joined a slow-moving line. We wondered if we would get to the front finally only to be told they too were full—did these others have reservations? We decided the man advertising must have vacancy and decided to go on to his place although it was nearly a kilometer past the place we were. Along the way we inquired at a few others—all *complet*. So we were thrilled to get two beds in the third floor dorm at *Cuatro Cantones*. (This was a rather new *albergue* that hadn't yet made it into most of the lodging lists and guidebooks.)

Like many, this *albergue* is run by a family. These families work together and work hard, doing everything required to take care of *peregrinos*, working particularly long hours during the peak seasons. The woman at the front desk registering pilgrims was the adult daughter of the man who was out drumming up business on the Camino earlier that day. She quickly and efficiently took care of a bunch of people who'd all come in at once, assigning spots, taking money, stamping *credenciales*, taking dinner reservations, and answering all kinds of questions. She provided laundry service—take a plastic tub, fill it with dirty clothes, and pay seven euros. Check back at the reception desk in a couple of hours— your bucket of dirty clothes will magically have become clean ones. I tried it—it works!

I was so glad to be here at this *albergue* right in the middle of the charming village of Belorado, not on the outskirts a kilometer back. It is tempting to want to stay in the first place you see and sometimes that is the best place. But if we'd stayed in the first *albergue* we would have passed through the village so early in the morning that we would have missed it! And so as soon as we'd showered and left our tub of laundry, I went exploring. There was a statue of John the Baptist in the church after his beheading, calmly holding his own head in the crook of his arm. I guess it was supposed to be inspiring but I thought it was a little creepy.

Behind the church was a steep rock face with visible entrances to some high caves that would have been very hard to access; they were inhabited at one time by hermit monks. But the thing that truly made this church unique was the backdrop for the steeple that towered over the church—the very typical flat steeple with three bells we saw all over Northern Spain with huge stork nests on all the highest points. That backdrop was higher yet than the steeple—a big, steep hill with the ruins of an ancient castle on top.

I stood on the ground in front of the church right on the Camino and looked up at those ruins. There was a big rocky peak on top of the hill and what appeared to be ancient bricks built on top of the natural rock. It was hard to tell where the rock ended and the bricks began, where the handiwork of men added to the handiwork of God, but it was clear that the rock wasn't entirely natural. A fortress had once towered over the village, maybe a thousand years ago. And I had to find a way to get up there!

I walked past the church surveying the route. I could see some people already there and it wasn't far. I walked in the direction of the caves and soon ran into a dead end, but in a few minutes time I was clearly on the dirt path behind the church leading up to the top and then directly over the church, looking down on it. It was an easy path with just a couple of switchbacks and soon I had an incredible view of the village and countryside. I was estatic—it was all so beautiful. I had to go back to the *albergue* and get Brian! His feet hurt but I convinced him it would be worth it and we went back up. He of course went to the very top of the ruins; I'm adventurous but terrified of heights.

We did a little more exploring of the town and found a marker that told us that nine hundred years ago, in 1116, Alfonso I "The Fighter" (King of Navarra and Aragon) gave this district a privilege that allowed it to celebrate a market, the most ancient market documented in the history of Spain. I understood the significance of this because I'd read (and also loved) the historical novel, *Pillars of the Earth,* by Ken Follett. This book about the construction of the great cathedrals of the medieval world mentioned these first markets and how a city could not have a market without a royal decree. These privileges could change the destinies of the people of these cities and were greatly coveted. Belorado became more alive to me because I knew the history. There was a large mural in the village depicting knights in their armor with shields and swords—it seemed almost real.

We'd bought tickets for dinner in the *albergue* and it was sold out; others went to restaurants nearby. We shared a table with a couple from Cleveland; he was Jewish and she was Catholic. We had a good conversation and then went off to bed.

We were sharing a room with probably twenty others in bunk beds spread out rather randomly. We had one pushed up against the wall, and there was a double bunk next to us with a very young couple walking the Camino on their honeymoon. There was no one on the bunk below them. They did a lot of giggling up there and pretty much kept to themselves—no one bothered them! There was a quiet older single woman in a single bed next to us and a Canadian man in a single bed on the opposite wall. Next to him was a bunk bed with a middle-aged Scandinavian couple. The pretty blonde woman, who was vivacious and friendly, stripped down to her underwear getting ready for bed. She was wearing a thong. I didn't realize they still made those instruments of torture. I had to admit she looked pretty good in it though, and I guess maybe she knew it, too.

The room we were in on the third floor of the very old stone building had a vaulted ceiling, with trees for beams, and some sections of trees propping up the middle, forcing us to duck under them in order to walk to the bathroom. We walked past several sets of bunkbeds to get there; a man in a lower bunk had hung two sheets to create a curtain giving him some privacy. The bathrooms had motion-detector lights requiring constant motion to keep them on. If you go to the bathroom at night, the incredibly bright lights first blind you then blink out stranding you in darkness; it pays to keep a sense of humor about it. I had such joy that night, laying awake with a heart filled with gratitude for the beautiful day I'd had, for the great gift this Camino was to me, and even for the sounds of all the living people surrounding me, for snoring, belching humanity.

Belorado to Villafranca Montes de Oca

E ggs for breakfast, always a treat, and then we once again joined the Camino river. We weren't far out of town when we ran into German Train Girl, who I learned also went by Leisa. She and I walked together for an hour or so while Brian walked on ahead. She seemed very young but was finishing up a Masters Degree in Psychology and then planning to go into counseling. She said she was going to take a break, though, before she continued her education—a few months to travel the world. "What do you call what you're doing now? The Camino? Isn't this traveling the world?" I asked her.

"No! This is not a vacation! And I'm going to need one after this!" She's right—it's not a vacation! It's hard work, but so rewarding. I had a sense while walking every day that the walking is my work, that it's valid, not frivolous. I had a job to do—to walk. I felt validated in my work, that it was productive and good and necessary. I had a purpose, an identify, I was a *peregrina*!

I'm grateful for the dignity that is given to *peregrinos*. It made me feel good to be greeted on the street by locals, to be wished a "*buen camino.*"An old man with a walker who I saw in a pharmacy nodded and said, "*Camino de Santiago*!" as if he were impressed. He then gestured to himself, patted his chest, repeated, "*Camino de Santiago,*" and then lifted his walker, tapping it on the floor. He laughed, making a joke about going on the Camino with his walker. I smiled and laughed with him, "*Sí, sí!*" We shared the friendly joke together.

It turns out that regardless of the amount of joy you experience in a night, if you don't sleep you're really tired the next day, and I wasn't the only one who listened to people snore all night. I did seem to find more humor in it that Brian did! So we stopped early that day in Villafranca Montes de Oca. The Hotel Anton Abad was originally a pilgrim hostel built in 1377 and was now a combination hotel/*albergue*. Like yesterday, the proprietor had also driven the pilgrim path soliciting business, and his efforts were rewarded. I figured that anyone so motivated would probably do a good job.

The hotel had tons of character. The halls were decorated with artwork and things from the medieval era and walking them gave you a sense of being there. Of course, the elevator was a later but welcome addition as was the plumbing in the rooms—these things didn't exist a thousand years ago. It turned out that something was wrong with the flush mechanism on the toilet. I went down and pantomimed the problem to the woman at the desk, and who came up to the room half an hour later and worked on it? The owner, the man who had been out drumming up business in the morning, who was to take our order at the restaurant that night, had probably cleaned some rooms and done who knows what else. He came into the room in a rush and then worked on the toilet with some frustration for twenty minutes, finally saying this was a good Spanish toilet, too bad they had to rely on the Chinese to make the flush mechanisms which were no good at all. The need to find a scapegoat to blame is as old as Adam, who blamed Eve. At least he was good-natured about it!

We also had a funny experience finding some lunch. We walked into a bar that was almost completely empty but it had a large menu posted on the wall advertising a *menú del dia.* We were really hungry, ready to order a big meal, but I kept wondering where all that food might come from—it was certainly not going to be whipped up by the bartender who was leaning on his elbows quietly visiting with another man. We made our choices and walked over to the counter to order.

"*No, no, comedor!*" the bartender answered, pointing at the door next to the posted menu and indicating that was where we were supposed to go. It did have a sign that said "*Comedor*" which we were to learn later was "Dining Room." We opened the door of the tiny, quiet bar into a large, loud room crowded with tables of diners and suddenly realized our mistake. So we went in and found a table where I ordered paella to start followed by a main course of fish. But when the huge plate of paella was brought out I cancelled the fish; there was no way I could eat any more than that. We left satisfied and went to take a short nap. I then spent most of the afternoon in the beautiful courtyard of the hotel reading, writing, praying, and just being. It was delightful.

I'd been reading, among other things, a biographical novel on St. John of the Cross. I was walking across Spain and reading about a Spanish mystic who lived five hundred years ago and is known today as one of the great Spanish classical poets. He was a Carmelite reformer, the priest who, together with his mentor, St. Teresa of Avila, founded the Discalced Carmelites. Discalced means "shoeless"—this new order would return to the austerity that monastics traditionally practiced. It was good to read this while I was on the Camino and to be reminded of how desperately the church of that day needed reform. Wealthy women had become nuns whose families financed lavish private apartments for them in the monastery with their own personal servants. John was strongly opposed in his efforts, at one point kidnapped, imprisoned, and nearly starved to death—by other monks! They whipped him in an effort to get him to repent. He eventually escaped and became a revered saint almost before his death. The Protestant Reformation was in full swing by then, but John managed to bring about much reformation within the church without splitting the church. As I visited so many churches along the Way, I wondered about their histories, the people who lived through the era John did. Did John of the Cross, the great Spanish mystic and writer, ever walk the Camino de Santiago? It was totally possible.

We went for a slow stroll through town late in the afternoon. We came upon a group of about eight middle-aged townswomen who met in the churchyard to play a bowling game with big wooden pins and a wooden ball. I'm guessing it was a regular weekly occurrence—they had a huge scoreboard with moveable wooden numbers and seemed to take it all very seriously. They were having fun and we were having fun watching. Brian rescued a little kitten that was stuck up in a tree. We went to a late dinner in the hotel restaurant (the owner was our waiter) and I ordered rabbit stew, which I regretted. It was too recognizable as a small animal and that night I had a bad dream about reaching up into a tree, grabbing a rabbit, and eating it live, fur and all. The dream was no doubt inspired by the kitten and I wished I could have had a pleasant dream about the women bowlers instead. I hope never to eat rabbit again.

Villafranca Montes de Oca to Almos de Atapuerca

I had that unpleasant dream early and was awake and bothered for a while. I spent some time praying myself back to sleep and then woke with a very pleasurable, in fact, beautiful, sense of peace. I had woken abruptly with a specific person in mind, a person I hadn't thought about in a long time. This person had betrayed me and deceived me years ago. I thought I had forgiven but when I woke, I knew I hadn't forgiven like I needed to. At least I hadn't up until that moment. I simultaneously knew that I hadn't adequately forgiven and at the same time, that real forgiveness was somehow accomplished in me at that moment by God's grace, and I was flooded with compassion for this person. I felt as if God's grace in the form of forgiveness had been poured into my life and kept pouring right through me into this other person's life. It made me think of Jesus' teaching about living water—flowing, flowing, flowing—constantly cycling and never being used up. The person who receives that living water will never thirst again.

I was so moved by this experience of grace. I hadn't been thinking about this person—why did this happen? I was filled with joy and went back to sleep praying I could sustain the holiness of this moment, the awe, the wonder. I knew this happened because of the thin place the Camino is, a place to touch the holy.

We were back in the hotel restaurant for breakfast at 7:00—the first ones there. After breakfast, we walked out the door and up a very steep hill. At the top is the *Alto de la Pedraja*, a memorial to local boys lost in the Spanish Civil War, dated 1936. The memorial features a dove of peace with an olive branch in its mouth. When will we learn that war never brings peace?

As we walked on Brian read the lyrics to Bob Dylan's *John Brown Goes off to War*. It's a story of a young man, proud to go off to fight, with a prouder yet mama caught up in the supposed glories of war, never imagining her son might not come home as a triumphant victor but as a broken man or maybe even not at all. It's a moving ballad, one that has been repeated countless times throughout history, a crippled and maimed veteran returning from battle with a handful of medals. War is hell. War is insanity. Our problems are never solved by war, and I pondered the sadness of it as we walked through the grey morning.

We ran into our Swedish friends again, Carin and Muna, and walked with them for a while. I learned that Carin is a musician who plays accordion and harmonica. Like me, she is a knitter, hiking in her knitted socks. She is married, but her husband has had back surgery and couldn't walk the Camino. He stayed home to take care of animals and plants and maybe grandkids. Her friend Muna is having trouble with her knee but is pressing on.

Lunch was in San Juan de Ortega, named after the disciple of Santa Domingo de Calzada. We stopped at a little café where several other *peregrinos* were gathered. There were no *bocadillos* so we settled for chips and orange juice. We sat an hour and visited with others and then the *bocadillos* came out, so we split one and had coffee. There was a woman there who looked like one of the oldest pilgrims I'd seen. She was busy telling people about an organization, the American Friends of the Camino, and asked me if I was a member. I hadn't heard of it and started to say, "No....," and she gruffly retorted, "Well, you should be!" I had to turn away so she didn't see me laugh. She was a tough old gal, recruiting by intimidation. Another pilgrim discreetly told me she'd been at the war monument the same time as him and had said, "1936? That's the year I was born!" She was eighty years old and a Camino regular. I was impressed.

In the afternoon we reached Atapuerca, a village where human bones dating back nine hundred thousand years were found in a cave, the oldest human bones ever found in Europe. The village has now become a UNESCO heritage site and I saw numerous signs depicting one of our earliest ancestors. It was moving to contemplate those early humans as we walked.

I know there are some Christians who believe the earth is only six thousand years old and that to believe otherwise is a stumbling block to their faith. They believe the Bible can only be taken literally, and therefore the world and all that is was created in six literal days only six thousand years ago. I have never had a problem believing in science and, in fact, understanding the incredible length of time God has been at work creating all that is doesn't hinder my faith; it only works to increase the awe and wonder I feel about it.

I see the first chapters of Genesis as a poetic depiction of Creation, a beautiful story that gives great glory to the Creator. It describes the gradual unfolding of what we see today, from "formless and void" through the development of all that is—the heavens and the earth, land and oceans, plants and living creatures. At first these creatures were primitive, living in the ocean, one-celled, but through processes which God developed became more complex and eventually adapted to be better suited to live and flourish in the environments that had also developed. All of this was God's work! But God didn't create by magic—poof, there it is. Yes, he spoke, but that too wasn't magic. God figured out how to do it all! The Creator set into place systems and mechanisms that would continue to unfold. There is much mystery involved and I believe God took great joy in it all, was in fact playful about it. At some point, in God's plan, in a mysterious way I don't pretend to understand, humankind came about. Genesis tells a beautiful story about God breathing his very own breath into this created being. It was at that point that humans became living souls.

I reveled in this, was excited contemplating this—that somehow I am, that somehow I came to be. I was grateful to have the privilege of living on this earth God created and rejoiced to think I was even at that moment walking across a little piece of it, five hundred miles of it. I had arrived in a village where, within sight of where I was walking, the bones of my ancestors from hundreds of thousands of years ago had rested. It was thrilling; I was awed and filled with wonder at it.

But we didn't stop in Atapuerca. We kept walking and for the first time planned to stay in a village a little off the Camino simply because we hadn't been able to get a reservation there. Olmos de Atapuerca was recommended in the guidebook as a worthwhile detour, and we jokingly called it Almost Atapuerca. I'd found a very unique place to stay that we thought looked interesting. When we continued walking on the highway that would take us to Olmos de Atapuerca rather than take the

Camino path which veered off to the left, a local man driving by immediately stopped to point out our mistake. It felt good to tell him we meant to do that; it was nice not to be wrong for a change! But it was a mile and a half further and the huge blister on Brian's right foot was hurting. I knew it and was proud of him for keeping a good attitude despite the pain. Thirty minutes after passing Atapuerca, we came to Olmos.

There is usually a bit of looking to find where we're staying unless it's a hotel with a big sign. This little town was totally deserted; we saw no one out. But walking along the sidewalk in town I saw something that made me laugh out loud. There was a yard full of chickens with a fence keeping them in, all except one little chick who was small enough to get through a hole in the fence and was running up and down the sidewalk, back and forth, while the big chickens inside were sticking their heads out the hole and clucking like mad. It was so hysterical I wanted to stand there and watch them, but Brian was way up ahead and was gesturing to me to hurry up. That wasn't the first time that had happened. He'd found our place and met our host who was waiting to get us checked in. So I hurried to catch up.

The *casa rural* (private home with a room to rent) turned out to be utterly charming. It was a newly built accommodation, a collaboration between two brothers with great artistic abilities and a commitment to environmental sustainability, a labor of love for sure. The woodworking in the house was sensational—excellent craftsmanship, beautiful natural furniture, an extremely unique stair railing, kitchen countertop, and cabinetry. It was a small place with maybe five or six rooms, and the owner let us know with his very limited English that for a small increase in price the top floor suite complete with sauna was available. We let him show it to us and couldn't resist. Everything about it was delightful. Whimsical leaded glass windows that looked like spiderwebs. A kitchen area that had colored wine bottles inlaid in a pattern within the plaster like stained glass, a skylight in the stairway opposite lighting it up. And, of course, the sauna.

After we got settled and showered, I wanted to go explore the village. I first visited the site of the Great Chicken Escape and laughed some more. Someone had been there and blocked the hole with a piece of ceramic roof tile. I assumed the runaway chick had been captured and stuffed back inside. I walked down the street and found the restaurant where we'd been told we'd be able to find some supper, the only restaurant in town. That was where I met Marina.

Marina was a German walking the Camino by herself. She was sitting at a table outside the bar, and I introduced myself. She was also staying at the *casa rural.* We visited for a few minutes, and the owner of the bar came out and communicated that though she was closed now, she'd be happy to get us a drink and hoped we'd come back for supper at 7:00 when she opened. She did this using no English, talking loudly and rapidly, but I understood her. We were back at 7:00 for supper, and a few minutes later Marina walked in alone. Brian and I invited her to join us. We were the only pilgrims in the restaurant that night, probably the only pilgrims in the village, although there were several locals there and even more when we finally got ready to leave. I can't imagine going to dinner at 10:00 but most Spanish wouldn't think anything of it. I'm up past my bedtime and way past being hungry!

We had a fun time ordering our supper as we had to do it completely in Spanish—every time we let an English word slip out the owner, a loud, fun-loving, extroverted woman, would say, "*No inglés! No inglés!*" Somehow, nevertheless, a nice meal was set before us. Even though this was a restaurant I felt like this woman was cooking for guests in her home; she took the orders, went behind the counter, prepared our plates, and served them with love and care. In fact, when it was time to leave she threw out her arms for a big hug—not what I typically experience at restaurants! We enjoyed dinner and our conversation with Marina. She was walking the Camino by herself and told us with a twinkle in her eye that her husband couldn't come because he had to stay home and make money so that she could walk the Camino. She said he was a few years away from retiring, and when he did, their dream was to travel through the western part of the United States in an RV and visit all the national parks. It's not a bad idea!

When asked why she was on the Camino, she said, "The Camino called out to me." I understand. It's difficult to put into words the strong feeling of that call, the compulsion, the knowing. She said she knew she had to do it and a year earlier, impulsively, she committed. She booked her plane tickets a year ahead, only telling her husband afterwards. She said that fortunately he was very supportive and that her Christmas present a couple of months later was the nice backpack she was carrying now. "I don't know why I chose those dates. I had no idea my mother would be stricken with cancer and I would lose her. It's just been two months and my heart is still broken; I miss her so much. She was so excited for me, and as I took care of her the last few months we often talked about the Camino. I would never have left her at the end. I would have cancelled this, but the dates were exactly right. How did I know that, way back last year?" The timing of the trip left Marina in awe. She said that God somehow knew she would be ready, in fact that it would be what she would need, and that knowledge brought her comfort as she continued to grieve her mother's death.

"Right before she died I asked her if she would be with me on the Camino, and she promised she would! But I have not felt her with me..." her voice faltered, and I felt her pain. We were silent a moment, and then Brian said quietly, "But your Camino isn't over yet." And we all pondered that.

Soon we finished our entrees, and Marina excused herself to go outside to smoke. "I'm sorry, I have to have it. I'll be quick!" She was gone for about two minutes, and when she returned I exclaimed on her speed. She pantomimed her ability to quickly inhale and smoke the cigarette and we laughed together. She said she wanted so badly to quit and hoped the Camino would help her do that. Brian asked her if she'd seen the movie, *The Way*. She hadn't. He explained that the movie is how most of the Americans we've met have found out about the Camino and that it was about a small band of *peregrinos* who walked together. The lone female smoked her way across the Camino, always claiming she'd give it up when she got to Santiago. She didn't, and she also came to realize that that wasn't what her Camino was about.

We ate our desserts, (it's hard to turn down when it's included with the meal!) paid and then hugged our hostess and headed back to the house.

It was about 9:00, and even though it wasn't a cold night, I wanted to try out the sauna in our room. I mean, we couldn't not! We had been shown how to turn it on and told it would take about fifteen minutes to warm up. But ten minutes in, the power in the entire house went out. I assumed we flipped a breaker, but what did I know? Did they even use breakers in Spain? And this was an environmentally friendly house—"*bioenergetique*"—what exactly did that mean? We had no phone number to call; as far as I knew, Marina and we were the only ones staying in the house. And even if we'd had a number, this was going to be tough to explain with our limited Spanish and an owner who spoke almost no English. It was very dark, and the only way we could get around was with the flashlights on our cell phones, which incidentally weren't going to get charged tonight. We'd have to get dressed and packed up in the morning with our cell phone lights, too. So much for the sauna!

Almos de Atapuerca to Burgos

And so we went to bed in the darkness of the night and the next day rose in the darkness of the morning. We'd made arrangements to leave together with Marina to find our way back to the Camino. We were a few minutes away from going downstairs to meet her when the lights suddenly came back on! When we went down, she said she'd found the breaker box and turned the power back on. She'd also got a pot of coffee going and was talking to another *peregrino* who we'd not yet met, John from Australia.

John had a story to tell of having gotten lost in the early morning hours of yesterday and walking a total of twenty-five miles to get here. He'd arrived around 6:00 while we were upstairs in our room. He'd heard us all leave to go to dinner but was too exhausted to budge from his bed to join us. He'd had nothing for dinner but a protein bar he was carrying with him. Breakfast was some pre-packaged pastries, yogurt, and coffee. Soon our small group of four set off cross-country—Marina and Brian dual-navigating with their respective GPS programs and John and I following their lead.

We walked up a big hill, stopping often to survey the lightening countryside and compare that to the GPS, enjoying the challenge and the conversation in the early morning. John had previously owned a sustainable energy company in Australia and we talked a bit about the windmills of Spain. We were walking up a rocky path when suddenly Marina pointed out a thick dark moving line also edging up the side of the path. It was a convoy of thousands of tiny ants forming a snakelike procession that was maybe two inches wide and ten feet long. Marina said, very deadpan, "Everyone wants to go to Santiago." She was so much fun. John and Brian were discussing *The Way*, which they'd both seen. John was a big guy and said he was like the Dutchman trying to lose some weight on the Camino. Brian laughed, told him about Marina and her cigarettes, and then said, "No joke, I'm an author," like the Irishman in the film.

Half an hour later we saw pilgrims ahead and rejoined the Camino. It was a happy day and we were enjoying the pilgrim camaraderie. I felt good and so joyful. My feet weren't hurting much, and Brian was doing pretty well; his blisters still bothered him, but today was a good day. And then suddenly Marina was struck with terrible pain in her knee. Brian gave her ibuprofen and John offered a tube of ointment that he said worked wonders. We slowed our pace and sympathized with her; I said a silent prayer. She was trying to be a good sport, but it was obvious she was in pain and also increasingly anxious. Another hour passed and we found a breakfast café with a yard full of hungry pilgrims enjoying coffee and particularly delicious Spanish tortillas; we happily stopped to join them. And it was here that we lost track of Marina; she left the café before we did, anxious to get on down the road.

We were heading to the big city of Burgos, and there was more than one way in, the official route or a longer route along the river which was recommended as more scenic. By the time we got there Brian's feet were hurting badly, and we didn't want to walk any further than we had to.

We stopped at a *farmacia* and stocked up on foot care items—Ibuprofen, Compeed, Vaseline, and Voltaren cream, which is what John had given Marina. Our knees were fine, but maybe it would help feet too. (I'm not sure it really did, but I began to faithfully rub Voltaren into my feet most mornings, followed by lots of Vaseline. On the Camino we treat feet very seriously.)

We walked for quite a while through the city even after stopping at the *farmacia* before finding our hotel. It was fabulous, right next to the very famous Burgos Cathedral. Checking in, we were offered an upgrade on our room; for ten euros we could have a view of the Cathedral. I'm glad we did; it was stunning. It was beautiful by day and magical by night, and we were able to lie in bed and see it fill our window. We had lunch in the Cathedral Square on a patio under some trees and I noticed Marcia at another table; I happily greeted her and hugged her. Marcia was the older woman from Alaska we'd been at two different *albergues* with—Casa Majica and Meruzabal. She told me she'd thought she'd just been dragging Charlie along, but now her feet were bad, she needed to stop, and she was surprised when he wanted to go on without her. So he had gone on with Robb, the man we'd all met at the same time in Villatuerta. I hadn't seen any of them for several days, and it was like a reunion of old friends; the Camino camaraderie quickly builds surprisingly strong connections.

As we'd walked through the city just before arriving at our hotel

in the historic part of town, we'd been passed by the *tren turistico*—
the little choo-choo train that tourists pile into to see the sites. I
noticed several familiar faces inside including Leisa, a.k.a. German
Train Girl, who gave us a slightly embarrassed wave as she went by.

After lunch we toured the Cathedral. I was more impressed by
the exterior than the interior. The construction of the building
was Gothic but much of the interior was later decorated in the
Baroque style. Yes, there was great beauty about it, but it seemed
gaudy and overdone to me—all that glitz, gilding, and gold
plating, an ostentatious display of wealth and grandeur fitting for
a king. And yes, Jesus was and is a king worthy of all of that, but
his life was a demonstration of poverty and self-sacrifice. I am,
frankly, not a fan of the Baroque style but was reminded when I
said so on social media that many others are. Mea culpa. I kept
wondering if perhaps it would have been better for all this money
to go to minister to the poor and realized that argument has
existed since at least the time of Christ. The Gospels tell a story of
a woman who poured out an entire bottle of expensive perfume
on Jesus in an act of extravagant worship. She was sharply
criticized by the disciples but commended by Jesus himself. I have
to remind myself that it is good to live in the tension between
those two poles. This edifice built to the glory of God has existed
for almost a thousand years and continues to be a reminder of
that glory. And so, like Mary, I need to "keep these things and
ponder them in my heart."

I did see our Swedish friends Carin and Muna as I walked into
one of the many chapels (twenty-one!) within the church and
greeted them warmly. Brian and I spent a quiet afternoon in our
room, and when we finally went out after dark, the square was
alive with crowds of people, restaurants with large sections of
outdoor seating, and live music. It was a fun party atmosphere. As
we'd enjoyed our lunch spot so much, right on the square, we

returned for supper and then went to bed with the window open enjoying the spectacular view of the white stone cathedral against the night sky. It was hard to close my eyes, but it was also hard to stay awake for long.

Burgos to Hornillos del Camino

We left Burgos behind early in the morning and I was a little sad we hadn't had more time there. It wasn't the first time I'd experienced that feeling. I was also a little anxious—today was the day we would enter what our guidebook called the "dreaded Meseta."

The Meseta was the middle section of the Camino. Pilgrims at *albergues* and cafes had been talking about the coming Meseta, and the guidebook also warned that while the Pyrenees and the area that we'd been walking through were physically difficult, the Meseta was emotionally and psychologically difficult. Psychologically difficult? We'd heard conversations about renting bicycles to quickly get through the Meseta or even taking buses to pass over it.

As we walked I couldn't see much difference. Of course there's no real line separating the country, but we had left the vineyards mostly behind and were now walking through farmland, through flatlands with row crops, wheat and barley and corn. There was less shade, but it was still pleasant walking. We shared a *bocadillo* and a peach in Tardajos.

I'd started reading *Hinds Feet on High Places* a few days before, the classic book by Hannah Hurnard, and it occupied my mind as we walked. It is a Christian allegory, a pilgrimage book. I was on a pilgrimage and this was a pilgrim book I'd never read. There is a story about that, a story I might have been a little ashamed of before, but I'm a little kinder to myself now and can laugh about it. Years before, probably twenty-five years in fact, a close friend, Susan, had tried to get me to read the book. I love fiction and it started off great—a girl named Much-Afraid, very tormented by her family, the Fearings, is called by the Good Shepherd to follow him on a long journey to the High Places. I remember enjoying the first part of the book, but my pleasure turned to disgust when she was introduced to her traveling companions, Sorrow and Suffering, and was asked to hold their hands. I remember throwing down the book in revulsion and horror—and telling my friend I refused to let those "witches" touch me. Months later I tried again, had the same visceral reaction, and gave up on ever reading the book.

I have come a long way since then and have had to acknowledge my very real fear of pain, sorrow, and suffering. No one likes sorrow and suffering, but as an Enneagram Seven, I now acknowledge a very deep seated fear of all kinds of pain and realize that facing it is the only way of conquering it. Running from it only gives it more power in my life. I thought at one time that faith in God would inoculate me from ever suffering or feeling pain, a very misguided belief. (If only I had more faith! If only I could believe more! And God only wanted me to learn to surrender and trust, rather than to work so hard at having faith.) So now I was reading Much-Afraid's story at last and had read past the point where she had taken her companions' hands and was enjoying the story greatly. I had reached the place where her name was changed to Acceptance-with-Joy. I walked that day in that new understanding, accepting with joy the beauty of the moment I was walking in, the beauty of the Camino, trusting that the Meseta would be a place of blessing and not a fearful place at all.

A man went by on a bicycle and gave me a thumbs-up which seemed to be almost a message from God, an AOK, a wink from heaven. It made me even more joyful. The sun was shining. The weather was perfect. I thought of the prayer I'd been praying written by a friend, Linda Tarman, back home.

This day, may I reside in a settled place
Even in the midst of the stir.
May I remember to look up periodically,
And around at the goodness that dwells here,
Wherever here is.
May I breathe in like it's the dawning
Of something new and lovely
Ready to pop out of the fertile grounding of the night
Into some luminous, crazy light.

This day may I lay aside my measuring stick
Which turns all living and inspiration into rule
And all promise into expectation.
May I release those who live
Sentenced by my judgments.
May they take flight to learn their own lessons
In the cloudy skies of growing,

As I myself must venture to do.

Fully present in my abiding today,
May I honor all past graces and grindings,
Miracles and manacles,
Which have nurtured me to freedom.

Today, may Your gentle and fierce love
Expand my heart to full capacity
And flow out unhindered
To drench the waiting world.

Here on the Camino, I was remembering to look up periodically and notice all the goodness that surrounded me. I was breathing in the dawning of something new and lovely. And I felt God's gentle and fierce love expanding my heart. I was experiencing the fruit of having prayed that prayer many times, and my heart felt very full.

We reached our destination, Hornillos del Camino, which looked like a little Wild West town. It was a tiny Camino village, one street wide, as everyone wanted to live on *Calle Mayor*, or Main Street. It looked like a Hollywood set for a cowboy movie. We had a reservation at a new *albergue* for a private room. Once again, the "*Complet*" sign was up when we arrived, but our room was waiting. It was a minimalist room for sure, a white box—white floor, white walls, white ceiling, and two twin beds with white spreads. There was a shared bathroom down the hall with multiple showers, sinks, and toilets—clean and spartan. We showered and took our laundry downstairs to wash. There was a machine but a line of tubs lined up to use it; it was easier and quicker to wash the clothes by hand in a big sink and then hang them on the line. We visited with some *peregrinos* sitting out in the yard and then walked down the street looking for something to eat—calamari and fries hit the spot. We spent the afternoon reading and then shared a pizza and salad before sleep. There was no gorgeous cathedral outside our window tonight—we were in a very, very different place but we were right where we were supposed to be, and that's a very, very good feeling.

Hornillos del Camino to Castrojeriz

We got an early start from the little Wild West town out into the hayfields of what looked very much like the Midwest where I've lived my entire life. As the sun was coming up behind us we looked to our left and saw five deer, not together but scattered all over the huge hilly countryside, serenely grazing the leftovers of that recently cut field. There was a peacefulness about the Meseta, particularly in the quiet of the early morning, and we walked in silence, breathing in the calm, breathing in the simple pastoral beauty, all the way to Hontanas, almost seven miles.

I remembered talking to a Jesuit priest back home as we were preparing for the Camino. He had already walked it and we asked him to share his insights. I told him I was somewhat familiar with the Ignatian exercises which are part of Jesuit spirituality and wondered if the Camino might be a good time to experience them. I was surprised when he laughed at my idea, saying the Camino itself would give us plenty of material to work through without having to look for more. I was beginning to understand how right he was.

We stopped in Hontanas at a café where there were lots of other pilgrims including the blond Scandinavian woman we'd met a week ago. She had bought a huge hunk of Manchego cheese and was passing out slices to all those around her. She said she and her friend had tried to rent bicycles to get through the Meseta but that it didn't work so they were stuck walking. She had a good attitude about it, was resigned to it. I'm guessing she was glad later, as I was, even though there were some challenging moments ahead for me that it was just as well I didn't know about.

Brian's feet hurt so badly that he took his boots off at the café. I was a little worried about him. He was trying not to complain, but it was clear he was distracted. He had a way of putting his head down and pushing through, but I knew he was suffering. We walked a little further and visited the local church. It was just a tiny little church, an old Catholic church, but they had removed several pews in the back and created a meditation area on the floor with candles, icons, Bibles laid out open in several languages, and big pillows to sit on. It blessed me to see the effort they were making to connect people with God, and I wanted to stay there for a while. Brian said, "Come on, let's go," and I knew he was anxious to get off his painful feet. He left and I lingered, and when I finally went out, he was nowhere to be found. We had a reservation in Castrojeriz, he knew I knew where, and I realized I was on my own for the time being.

Months before I had told some women from my church about our plans. I still remember one comment from a woman who would say she has a good marriage but she wasn't sure she and her husband could stand that much exclusive time together. I understood what she meant. I have always understood that to expect one person to meet all your emotional needs is a recipe for disaster. My marriage is strong and I also enjoy spending time with other people and time alone. We'd talked before the Camino about doing some "alone" days. And so walking alone that day was also a joyous experience even though it wasn't prearranged. I was able to dawdle and explore and had a delightful time.

On the next section of trail I seemed to be totally alone, and it was truly beautiful. The sun was shining, the temperature was perfect, I could smell the newly cut hay, and I was so aware of the presence of God and how God delighted in the day, too. I walked past what I guessed were the remains of an ancient castle—the corner of a stone wall, an oddity, four feet wide and towering twenty feet or so into the sky. I had to scurry up the remains of a retaining wall to get to the "castle"—out in the middle of a deserted field, no marker or sign to tell me what it had been, who had lived there, the story of that ancient and romantic castle. I walked around it, pondered it, and imagined. My mind devised some stories of its own. Later I found a mention in a guidebook of the remains of an old mill somewhere in the vicinity, but since it is inconclusive whether these are the same ruins, it will remain a castle in my mind until I am corrected otherwise.

The path eventually turned into a road lined with trees and I noticed for the first time some fall colors in the green trees. I was caught up in the change of color when a *peregrina* passed me walking fast. It wasn't until I recognized the familiar German Dautier backpack that I yelled, "Marina!" She turned around, realized who she'd passed, and came back for a hug. She was wearing a knee brace, had seen a doctor in Burgos instead of the cathedral, and was back on the trail, full speed ahead to Santiago! I told her I had prayed for her this morning, which touched her. We chatted as we walked and arrived at San Antón in a few minutes time.

San Antón had been a huge monastery and a well-known fourteenth-century hospital for Camino pilgrims, now in ruins. (Hospital, hospitality, hostel, hotel—all these words have the same origins.) It was impressive and had no doubt been incredibly impressive seven hundred years ago. An *albergue* exists even to this day—an *albergue* without electricity and, I heard, questionable plumbing. Marina and I went into the ruins which were breathtakingly beautiful—soaring stone arches and windows without glass, but the blues, greens, and browns of the trees and sky seen through the windows were far more beautiful than any stained glass could ever be. Maybe the next time we walk the Camino we'll stay here? Ah, probably not, it sounds romantic, but I do enjoy the comforts of modernity.

And when we went back outside, (although inside the monastery was really outside) another surprise—there was Carin, trying to decide if she wanted to stay there. She told me Muna had stayed behind in Burgos with a bad knee and was seeing a doctor today. Carin and I talked a bit while Marina walked on. I then made my way on my own, at my own pace, on down the road to Castrojeriz. I had a slightly unpleasant experience—stopping to use a toilet at a bar along the way. It was a sort of "outside" bar, with tables sitting around on the ground and a little building out by the road that was marked "toilet." There was a sign that the toilet was for customers only, and I usually respected that request, but it was the only place around and I didn't want to stop long enough to buy a drink I didn't want, so I made an exception. When I came out and was slinging my pack on my back, the owner came over in his dirty white t-shirt and angrily confronted me. The truth was that despite the fact that I didn't want or need a drink or a snack, I also only had a euro fifty in my pocket. I had more money in my pack but I didn't want to take even more time to dig it out just so I could use the toilet. It was also not a real welcoming environment, just two customers sitting at a table and the proprietor standing behind the bar with a glare. And so the man got ugly, was in my face, asking why I couldn't come have a drink, he had drinks for just a euro, and on and on. I thought of Much-Afraid and I refused to be intimidated. I took the euro out of my pocket and said, "Here is a euro for your toilet. I don't want a drink." He started to argue, then to give it back, and finally put it in his pocket and turned away, while I clipped my pack and left his establishment. I was proud of myself for not over-apologizing. Yes, I was sorry I'd ignored his sign. This was not an experience typical of the Camino—most everyone was kind and accommodating and I refused to let this spoil my mood. And so, like Scarlet O'Hara, I tripped on down the road, saying "Fiddle-dee-dee!"

I was walking down a long, straight, beautiful, tree-lined road, and I could see Castrojeriz in the distance for a long time. It was exciting to approach, with a huge Renaissance-era cathedral at the end of that tree-lined road and the remains of a medieval-era castle on a mountain looming over it. My anticipation grew as I got closer—it was hard to believe this was real and not a fanciful piece of art. The church was five hundred years old but the castle a thousand. I found myself wondering what the castle had looked like when the church was being built. It was a picture of contrasting kingdoms, the old passing away, the new has come. "The kingdoms of this world, they have become the kingdoms of our Lord and of his Christ and he will reign forever and ever." The words of Handel's Messiah, taken from the words of Isaiah the prophet.

When I finally arrived at the church, I couldn't resist going in, and I was sad then to realize it was no longer a church but a museum. So I went on, left the church behind, and focused on the castle looming above me. There was a road that looked like it might be the way up—a sign that said *"Castillo"* and an arrow that was a little confusing—it pointed to the left when it clearly should have pointed ahead, but I was anxious to get to the hotel and meet up with Brian. I walked and walked and walked—nearly two kilometers through this little town with a population of six hundred. It was really spread out, but I enjoyed walking the streets and seeing the town.

I found Brian at Hotel Jacobus, a very cool old hotel, sitting in their beautiful garden reading and enjoying some olives and tapas. I sat down and ordered a salad. He'd had a lot of pain getting there, said he wished he'd been able to be more present to the moment but that his feet preoccupied him. He was making the best of it, however, and I was both proud of him and felt bad for him as well as grateful for the wonderful day I'd experienced. I told him I'd gone in the cathedral turned museum and we both agreed that neither of us wanted to walk an additional four kilometers to go back there. We had been in a lot of churches turned museums and there was a sadness about that.

After I'd showered and taken a little siesta, I wanted to try to get to that castle! I walked back to where I'd seen what I thought was the turnoff. I started up the switchbacks only to realize within about ten minutes that this road wasn't taking me where I thought it would. I did find a bunch of strange dwellings built into the side of the mountain. I thought they were homes but learned later they were *bodegas* where families traditionally stored wine and other preserved foods. I'm not sure that some of these particular *bodegas* hadn't been converted into some rustic accommodations; one was locked up tight and I could hear a dog barking inside. I shortcutted down from that spot on the mountain and back towards the *Calle Mayor* right behind another church, this one still in use, the local parish. I came upon four young teenagers, three boys and a girl, perhaps all thirteen-year-olds, horsing around and acting like typical thirteen-year-olds. Perhaps they could tell me the way up to the castle!

And so I asked. "*Hola. Hables inglés?*" They all looked at one another, laughed nervously and said, "*No.*" But one of the boys puffed out his chest, and said, "*Sí.*"

"Oh great," I said, "can you tell me how to get up to the castle?" A look of horror crossed his face—and I realized he didn't speak English as well as he'd let on.

The girl, a pretty girl with long black hair and gorgeous dark eyes, took a deep breath and gave it a shot. "Up....the way, street," she struggled and gestured. We all volleyed a few phrases back and forth; everyone participated and had a good time.

But they couldn't tell me how to get to the castle, so I gave up, said, "*Gracias,*" and went on.

I was loving Spain and I was loving this little town. A man on an ancient all-white bicycle passed me—I think it had been spray-painted. I could only see him from the back but he was dressed in a way that you don't often see on the Camino, like a Tibetan, with a long white embroidered jacket and a tall, round, flattop hat, with short braids hanging below it. I walked a little further and found Marina sitting at a café. She asked if I'd been to the *Hospital de Almas* yet—the Hospital of Souls. She encouraged me to keep walking just a bit further on the *Calle Mayor* and I would find it. When I got there the white bicycle was leaning against the side of the building, and a sign invited me in. I opened the door and entered the Hospital of Souls.

I entered into another world, a quiet room of contemplative tranquility. It was a small room, a room dedicated to meditation and serenity. There were candles, fountains, the sound of running water. Pictures of beautiful places, quotes designed to pull you out of the busy world just outside into the gentle world of the interior, the world of the soul. It was a small room but just beyond was another room, another spot to sit and meditate, and then another and another. It reminded me of the different chapels in a big Catholic church. I slowly walked from room to room quietly breathing in the spirit of the place. The Tibetan bicyclist was sitting outside in a garden decorated just as beautifully and creatively. He didn't acknowledge me, and I continued to tiptoe around and explore. I walked from room to room and even upstairs in this very old building that exuded such peace. Another man who appeared to be a *peregrino* was also there, and after fifteen or twenty minutes we both reached the place we'd entered to leave and saw the white bicycle had been brought inside the front room. The other man reached for the door and found it locked. We'd been locked inside, and the Tibetan was gone.

There was a brief moment of confusion. I was locked inside the Hospital of Souls with a stranger? Brian and I had commented on the use of door locks in some of the places we'd stayed—being issued two or sometimes three keys to get to our room—an outside door key, an inside door key, and sometimes a key between those two, a key to a suite of rooms or a hotel within a hotel. It wasn't too difficult to get used to using the keys to get in, but it was odd you also had to use the key to get out. What if there was a fire or another emergency? Building codes in America would never have allowed such a situation. It made me a little careful about knowing where our keys were rather than just tossing them down. But it was also a good practice of being mindful, living in the moment. I mean, isn't it generally a good thing to know where your keys are?

But here we were now, locked in, what were we going to do? The man and I looked at one another, never speaking, and then he reached down to turn the skeleton key that was providentially sticking out of the keyhole. How did the Tibetan leave, locking the door, with the key in the keyhole on the inside? I didn't know, but now we were out. I felt a little bad about leaving the Hospital of Souls open and unattended. But it was another example of the Camino mysteriously providing whatever it was we needed.

Brian and I had a great meal that night sitting out on the terrace under a night sky. He was concerned about his worst blister, the huge one on the ball of his foot extending up between his toes. He now thought new socks would help. He'd brought very heavy mountain-climbing Smartwool socks and regretted it. A small thing like buying socks gets complicated in a small town in Spain when you are committed to doing everything on foot. We'd been so lucky to find the large sporting goods store to buy my new insoles, the store that was touted as the only one right on the Camino. Would there be a similar provision for socks for Brian? I googled "hiking store Castrojeriz" on my phone and came up with a "*Bazar de Peregrinos*" right here in Castrojeriz. It was a dot on a map—there were no reviews or description, only a Facebook mention and hours—9 to 5. If only we had looked for it earlier in the day when we had plenty of time to shop. It would mean a late start in the morning but it was worth a try.

Castrojeriz to Itero de la Vega

The address we had for the *Bazar de Peregrinos* was right on the Camino; we reached it no more than three minutes after leaving the Hotel Jacobus, which had been a special place. We had loved sitting in the garden, eventually eating supper under the stars. There was a balcony right off our room where we'd hung the laundry after washing it in the bathroom sink. We were leaving after the sun was up and it was so pleasant to look out over the countryside as I gathered and folded. I heard owls hooting and roosters crowing amidst the constant twitter of little birds, the soundtrack of God's world—so peaceful. I could have sat on the balcony for the entire morning, but we left to be at the *Bazar* when it opened.

We had found the address easily but no sign of a store, just a long row of what appeared to be boarded-up buildings. We walked a block in either direction looking for it. I climbed a long set of stairs up to an *albergue* where a few lingering *peregrinos* were preparing to depart for the day and tried to ask if anyone knew where the store was, but my poor Spanish was met with blank stares. It was 9:00 and the town was all boarded up. I was guessing that the store, if it had ever existed, had gone out of business. Just then a taxi pulled up and a man got out dressed in traditional

German lederhosen—short leather pants with suspenders. He was an older *peregrino* from Germany who spoke some broken English, enough to explain that the taxi driver had brought him to the only hiking store for miles around from a town we'd walked through yesterday. He showed us the sole of his worn boot; it had come completely loose and was flapping with each step; they had to be replaced. He was a little sad as he had had those boots for years and was sorry to give them up. He's walked sections of the Camino every year for many years. We were glad the man had shown up—surely the taxi driver would not have brought him here if there was no store? We had been on the verge of going on.

At 9:05 a door across the street opened and an old man slowly hobbled towards us. He was obviously a local and when he approached I tried to ask him if he knew anything about the store. Brian said, "Peri, he's the proprietor." Oh. It took another five minutes for him to unlock a heavy metal door, remove metal shutters from a big window, and haul some clothing racks out on to the sidewalk, enough for us to get in the packed store. We waited until he gestured it was okay to come in. The *Bazar de Peregrinos* was a fully loaded hiking store with top quality shoes, clothing, and who knows what else. It was so fully loaded that only the proprietor knew where everything was. He looked at the German's shoes and pulled some boxes off the shelf for him to consider. We found some good socks on a nearby rack. The German bought new boots and a tube of Superglue to try to repair the old ones, and after paying we all sat outside together. Brian changed his socks and the German, in his new boots, worked at gluing the old ones that he planned to tie to his pack because he just couldn't stand to part with them. We bid him "*Buen Camino*" and were off for our day.

Five minutes later, we were also bidding Castrojeriz goodbye when I saw a sign marked "*Castillo*" and an arrow pointing up; I immediately understood that this was the road I was looking for yesterday, the road of switchbacks that would take me to the castle. It was almost two kilometers past the road I'd tried yesterday and suddenly yesterday's confusing sign with the arrow pointing left made perfect sense. And I so wanted to go! Brian and I decided to go our own ways again. I felt a twinge of guilt, but I knew I would want him to follow his heart if the roles had been reversed. I started up the road to the *castillo* and he headed on to Itero de la Vega where we had a reservation.

It took me twenty-five minutes to walk the switchbacks and I found myself wishing I could have left the heavy backpack behind, but the views were incredible and well worth the detour. I walked through the area where the stone for the castle had been quarried and then into the deserted ruins. There had been some restoration work done and signs to indicate how the castle had looked in its glory days. It was quite an impressive edifice and I spent some time exploring and overlooking the huge valley below. I spent as much time as I wanted there and was back to the place Brian and I had parted an hour after I'd left, ready to leave Castrojeriz, one of my favorite towns on the Meseta. I left wishing I could stay, consoling myself with the hope of coming back but knowing there were more adventures ahead.

There are so many views from the Camino stamped in my memory and I'm so glad I took the time to breathe in and really see and absorb the panorama that stretched before me as I left Castrojeriz. I could see the trail ahead for a long, long way stretching straight ahead across the flat prairie, a few scattered trees along the trail but mostly a wide open expanse. On the horizon a huge hill, the trail crossing at an angle. It looked like a beast of a hill and yes, when I got there, it was indeed a beast. It was the *Alto de Mostelares*, a hill with a name. I stopped a couple of times to rest, got passed by a group of three young men, and finally arrived at the top, out of breath and sweaty but feeling triumphant.

The three men were sitting in a shelter at the top eating oranges. Two others were lying on the ground. I sat for a few minutes to have a snack and get my breath and was offered an orange. While I was there, another young man, tall and skinny, staggered up yelling profanities as he collapsed on the ground. "What the (blank)! What the (blank)! (Blank)! That (blank)ing killed me!" He reminded me of a toddler with his under-developed vocabulary. He was also probably embarrassed that his buddies had arrived so much sooner than he had.

Coming down the other side of the *Alto de Mostelares* was steep too, made easier by a paved walk. Then a long flat straightaway where I passed a lot of people, walking through farmland, and seeing a green John Deere combine which made me feel right at home.

I then approached a surprisingly large crowd of people sitting at a shelter along the road. They turned out to be a group of Americans on a bus tour, driving the Camino route and walking short portions some days. As I've said before, there are many ways to do the Camino, and these people were happy to be having this experience. The German we'd met at the hiking store that morning was there too, changing his shoes. The glue had dried and he wasn't happy with the new ones—"the old are better." I complimented him on his lederhosen and he said, "They're old like me," with a big toothy grin. I took his picture and hugged him. We were old friends; I'd met him early this morning. Camino camaraderie.

I walked on and an hour later passed a thirteenth-century hospital for pilgrims that still functions as a small *albergue* for those willing to forego electricity. It was lit with candles and full of icons. It would have been interesting to stay there and I told myself maybe next time. I crossed a river into Palencia talking to an Irish chef and a few minutes later entered Itero de la Vega. Our hotel was a Wild West saloon; we were staying in Room 3 upstairs and I fully expected Miss Kitty to arrive any minute. I found

Brian eating a sandwich in the bar, and I joined him and ordered one for myself. As I sat there I rejoiced that I hadn't even thought about my feet or wanted to take my shoes off—what a huge relief! But I was sad to hear that Brian's were still bad. He'd changed his shoes that day too, wore his trailrunners that were supposed to be his alternate pair, and carried the boots.

There was a couple from Texas sitting nearby and we struck up a conversation. He said they'd walked the Camino a couple of years before, actually just the beginning and the end but had skipped the Meseta and had now come back to finish. We talked about feet and shoes and he showed me his heavy leather boots. "Best boots in the world, wouldn't wear anything else." I told him I'd had some trouble early on but that the new insoles I'd bought seemed to make a big difference. "Really? I might have to get some because my feet are killing me!" That was surprising since he'd just told me how great his boots were. He then confessed they were both beat and had called a taxi that was going to take them somewhere, anywhere, away from this pain and misery. The woman put her head down on the table in despair. I never saw them again.

We spent some time in the afternoon sitting on the big patio outside in the sunshine. I felt joyful, rich and satisfied. That night we had a hearty pilgrim supper of asparagus, fried pork and fries, with flan for dessert.

Itero de la Vega to Frómista

I was awake a lot in the night. It was pleasant; I experienced joy in the presence of God and much peace. I thought about how often I was afflicted with stress and anxiety and a sense of impending doom and how much better it was to live with a constant sense of unfolding grace. I thought about Dallas Willard's thoughts on grace, that God's grace is always available, and that we are to "burn grace like a 747 burns jet fuel."

I heard noise in the hall. It was 1:48 am. Loud whispers in Spanish. Not *peregrinos*! No pilgrim stays out that late.

I thought about the fact that medieval pilgrims didn't walk the Camino de Santiago because of the walk—they walked because it was the only way to get to Santiago for the blessing. But maybe the blessing wasn't really ever at the great cathedral, but in the transformation that occurred as a result of the walk. The way is made by walking indeed. And I felt so compelled to walk it too.

If nothing else, the Camino forces you to slow down, to slow way down, to reduce your possessions to a bare minimum. It seems like I am always looking for something I've lost at home—a book, my keys, my phone. It exasperates me, I acknowledge my scatteredness. (I'm an Enneagram Seven—of course I'm scattered.) But on the Camino I lost nothing! It was because I had so little and everything had a place. My pack was packed every morning in pretty much the same way, and I quickly learned how important that was. Once I packed it a little differently, and as soon as I put it on, I felt a shoe poking me in the back. I had to empty it out and start over. I say "pretty much the same way," because of course it was not packed in exactly the same meticulous way as Brian packed his, the guy who was so impressed by the train leaving the station exactly on schedule!

It was now 2:30 am. I felt love and compassion for the owners of this hotel, a father and son, maybe forty and seventy, working hard to check people in, serve food and drinks, no doubt cooking in the restaurant as well as all the other unseen things required. I said a prayer for them and for all those who serve pilgrims on the Camino and provide all the things we need. I prayed for Brian and particularly for his feet. I felt sad that these blisters were robbing him of the joy I was experiencing. I coughed a few times. A cold coming on? No! I told myself to be at peace and then told God I'd enjoyed our time together but please help me get to sleep now. I asked nicely which you would think would elicit an immediate answer, but evidently it doesn't work that way. I coughed some more and laid there a while longer.

I didn't get as much sleep that night as I would have liked, but I refused to let it bother me. I was enjoying my nighttime wakefulness. I was determined to enjoy it all and consciously live in the moment.

We were on the road at 8:00 after a tiny breakfast in the dark bar—coffee and a prepackaged pastry. Brian had abandoned his boots, leaving them and three pairs of heavy socks in the hotel room. I hoped someone who could use them. He wore the new socks and his old trailrunners and he was miserable as we started out. He was moving slowly with his head down. We didn't talk. I prayed silently for him—what else is there to do? We arrived in Boadilla in about two hours—five and a half miles. He said it was the worst day of the trip—that his foot hurt so bad he thought he would throw up. We found a coffeeshop, he took off his shoes, and I got him coffee and a potato omelet and more Ibuprofen. He put on some more Compeed. The next four miles were better. I asked him to quote some Dylan lyrics, trying to distract him, and he did, all the way to Frómista where we checked into a nice hotel, the Doña Mayor.

The cough I'd experienced the night before? Yes, it was the beginning of a cold and I had coughed throughout the morning, too. I had told Brian yesterday I thought he needed a day off to rest his feet and he'd quickly dismissed that idea. Today, checking into the sunny room at the Doña Mayor of Frómista with the comfortable balcony, I had even more reason to insist—now it wasn't only for him but for me, too. He objected, saying we had a reservation down the road. I countered back with the suggestion that it could be canceled. He finally gave in; I was thrilled and went down to the lobby to make the arrangements.

The Doña Mayor turned out to be the perfect place for an extra day. The room was comfortable, the balcony overlooked a sunny courtyard, but the best thing was the tender loving care administered by the two women who ran the hotel whom I am convinced were actually Camino angels. One of them threw my filthy laundry in a machine and when it was washed gave me a hanging rack and showed me where to set it outside to get the best exposure of the sun. They fixed us a wonderful meal—carrot and pumpkin soup and then vegetable lasagna full of sautéed spinach and onions, lots of cheese, and surprisingly, raisins. After lunch we slept, and slept some more, all afternoon, going downstairs that night for a light supper and then back to bed. I had just a little cold when we had arrived and never would have insisted on staying a second night on that account—it was a welcome excuse to use to get Brian to stay for the sake of his feet. But then it did get worse. I had a sore throat and laryngitis, and I'm convinced that the day off was providential for my health too.

The next day I stayed in bed till a glorious 9:00 and then went downstairs to bring some breakfast up to Brian. After a leisurely morning, he put on his flip-flops, and we slowly padded two blocks to the *Iglesia de San Pedro*. The church was a big Gothic building from the fifteenth century. It was an active church but also housed a museum of church artifacts and artwork, particularly the altarpiece stolen from *Santa Maria del Castillo*, recovered somehow after a robbery in the 1980s. There was a caretaker, a friendly man who was enthusiastic about showing us the beautiful things there. We spent considerable time in the tiny one-room museum, and it was a special treat to examine the paintings of the altarpiece close up. They were very detailed paintings of Gospel scenes.

The depiction of the Last Supper showed thirteen men gathered around a table, Jesus in the center. Across from him was Judas, seen from the back, the moneybag hidden behind him. Peter and John were on either side of Jesus, and James next to John, already wearing his pilgrim hat and Camino scallop. John was leaning on Jesus' breast, as the Scripture says; he also had his finger stretched out touching the side of the skinny lamb laid out in a bowl in the center of the table, the dinner they were about to eat. This puzzled me, what could it mean? Surely John wasn't tickling the lamb in the ribs? It struck me as comical, but a friend I shared it with, a friend evidently more spiritually astute than I was, said he was prophetically touching the side where Jesus would be pierced. Oh, yes.

Another painting showed Jesus being arrested in the Garden. There were six figures crowded into the painting—Jesus in the center, the arresting Roman soldier with his arm stretched out to seize Jesus while Judas kissed his cheek. Peter was there, sword in hand, another Roman soldier right behind him. Peter had just severed the ear of Malchus the servant, who lay stunned on the ground. And Jesus held the ear in his hand, his only concern at that moment to bring healing.

These paintings were designed to teach people the stories of the Gospel, and they were beautiful. I loved seeing them and the crucifixes and statues and other religious art. We finally left and walked slowly another two blocks to the older *Iglesia de San Martin*, a smaller tenth-century Romanesque church. This church had had significant restoration work done so it actually looked newer than the fifteenth-century church. The hotel we were staying in, the Doña Mayor, was named after the widow Doña Mayor, the benefactor who provided for the construction so long ago of the original church. All these stories from another time—how I would love to know more, to have known the people. Later, looking at my pictures, I noticed how a picture I took of my Camino angel back at the hotel resembled a picture I'd taken of a statue in *Iglesia de San Pedro* of Mary, the mother of Jesus. Mysterious.

Brian was ready to get back to the hotel and off his feet. I walked back with him, got our *credenciales*, and took them back to St. Martin's for pilgrim stamps. I then explored the city a little more, finding my way to both an ATM machine and a *farmacia* where I did some shopping—two more packages of Compeed, some ibuprofen, cold medicine, antacids, and bandaids. The pharmacist also talked me into buying his specially concocted blister salve. It didn't take much persuasion; I was ready to try anything. I saw a French pilgrim pulling a little two-wheeled wagon with a strap cinched around his waist, loaded down with cooking supplies and food; this pilgrim was dedicated to fine dining. I was plenty satisfied with the food we were getting all along the way. We rested in the afternoon, but my cold continued to get worse. I was grateful for the day off, wondering if I would be ready to go again in the morning. My voice was almost gone. My sore throat seemed worse. Texting with a friend from home, she told me "what you need is tea with lemon and honey." I told her it sounded wonderful, but I had no idea where to get it or how to ask for it. Communication was so difficult with our limited Spanish.

I went down to the lobby to let them know that we were indeed planning to check out in the morning. And my Camino angel heard my pathetic croaking voice and said, "Oh....I make you....I make you special drink. I make you tea with lee-mon and, how you say, ho-nay?" She was so sweet it made me want to cry. She went into the kitchen and came out a few minutes later with a piping hot cup of the nectar of the gods. It was so delicious and soothing and I felt the love and kiss of God in it. Again, the Camino provided exactly what I needed or, more explicitly, God provided exactly what I needed to continue the Camino.

Brian wanted to go out to eat in the evening and went and found some pizza. The tea was enough for me and I enjoyed quiet time in the room sitting with Jesus in meditation, simply being in God's presence. I slept well despite a lot of coughing and felt ready the next morning to continue. We had taken a sabbatical from our sabbatical and it felt like a long time since we'd been on the Camino. I missed it. I was more than ready to fall back into the Camino river.

Frómista to Carrión de los Condes

e started out early in the dark. We had a good morning walking in the shade along a river. This is the part of the Meseta that gets such a bad rap. The Camino follows what the guidebook calls a "soul-less *senda*" in this area, a pea-gravel sidewalk alongside a major roadway. When possible, there are alternate routes that are recommended—more scenic but frequently adding some distance. We did choose the alternate route that day and I was determined to enjoy it, to not let the Meseta get me down. I concentrated on breathing in the love, mercy, and healing presence of God. We stopped after eight miles and had some mussels and a drink in the town of Villacázar de Sirga next to the magnificent thirteenth-century Templar church, *Santa Maria la Virgen Blanca*. The church was ornate and the altarpiece was spectacular. It was even more spectacular when we put a euro in a box to turn the spotlights on it.

We had four more miles to Carrión de les Condes where we had booked a room in an old monastery renovated into a hotel, but after lunch we both suffered. Brian's foot hurt and my throat hurt and I was coughing a lot. I was uncomfortable and tired, but he was miserable. And knowing he was suffering made me suffer more. I was tired of him feeling bad. It seemed the day off didn't really cure either him or me. I felt discouragement creeping in. We both grew very quiet—what was there to say? And anyhow I needed to rest my voice. I walked ahead of him for a while; we both needed to be alone. I talked to God and tried to discern what love would do.

We walked straight through town without stopping to look around. Brian was desperate to be finished. Our hotel was on the far side of town, really past it. We arrived, showered, rested, and went to eat in the hotel restaurant. It was very good food—Brian had black pudding and I had gazpacho. But I felt demoralized. I knew my cold contributed to my discouragement, I was tired. I couldn't help thinking we had entered John Bunyan's "Slough of Despond" and were stuck. All bogged down. Stuck in the stupid Meseta. Not making much progress, only twenty-one miles in the last three days. It helped to remind myself that the Slough of Despond was an allegory, that we were living the allegory, that the whole Camino de Santiago was an allegory for life. No, we weren't making much progress right now, but I kept telling myself, "This is just an allegory! We are going to make it!" I knew we could quit the Camino any time we wanted and I also knew we wouldn't. I was oddly encouraged in the midst of my discouragement.

I felt bad, too, that I hadn't seen much of the town, Carrión de los Condes, which was a major stopping point in medieval times. There were so many interesting things we had walked right past earlier and that pained me. I didn't want to miss any of it! But I was sick which made me tired. I needed some cough medicine. So visiting the *farmacia* was my evening outing, and I meandered through some interesting parts of town getting there and enjoyed the Old World beauty. The lack of language is intimidating; the lack of a voice complicates things even further. I entered the pharmacy tentatively and a pretty young woman approached me with a smile.

"*Hable inglés?*" I whispered hopefully.

The girl said, "A leetle, I try."

"I need something for my throat and a cough." I gestured at my throat.

"*Qué?*"

"I have a cough!" I enunciated more clearly.

She replied, "I don't know what is coff."

So I showed her. I coughed a little. But a little cough turned into a long episode. I stood there coughing while she said, "Oh, I know," and ran to the back room to get the correct medicine.

I came home with some medicated "*zum-zums*" which are not "*masticables*" but things you suck on, up to 4 times a day. There was a tablet to dissolve in water and drink once a day. (When I showed Brian back in the room he asked me, "But do you drink it in the morning or at night—will it put you to sleep or keep you up?" A detail I had neglected to ask, but I mixed some up then and there and drank it down—my version of living dangerously.) I got some Halls. I also had some powdered cold medicine that I got in yesterday's *farmacia*. I didn't know if I could take it on top of the other stuff, but I decided I would if I felt bad enough! I think the cold medicine had an ingredient that is no longer sold in America. Decifering pharmaceuticals in Spanish adds another level of complexity. But the kindness of the woman in the pharmacy was an encouragement. Lord, help me to remember that kindness is always encouraging!

Carrión de los Condes to Calzadilla de la Cueza

We both slept nine hours after having napped in the afternoon and then skipping supper. When I woke I was amazed; I hadn't coughed once in the night. And my throat and voice were better. I was so grateful. We had a very nice breakfast in a lovely dining room—good fruit, bread, eggs, coffee, cheese. We sat with an American woman from San Francisco and had good conversation. She told us this was her second time on the Camino, that she had come a couple of years earlier as she was grieving the loss of her mother. She walked for a couple of weeks and then one day said to herself, "I think my mother would rather I'd gone to Paris." And so she quit the Camino and went to Paris for the duration of her trip; now she was back to give it another go.

We walked through the Meseta that day under overcast skies. Brian had allowed me to bandage his foot, to change the Compeed. It was a complicated process because the blister extended up between his toes and required several carefully sized pieces of Compeed. His feet seemed a little better today, but nevertheless, we were only walking ten and a half miles. We walked on an absolutely flat, absolutely straight road, a Roman road that had been built through a bog. It was amazing to think of the amount of fill material that had been brought in from a long distance to build up the base, a base that was still intact two thousand years later. The Roman reputation for infrastructure is well deserved. They do bridges and roads like no others ever have.

I watched a hawk circling above us for a long time, using that keen vision her creator gave her, seeking out movement below, her morning prey, her breakfast. I remembered an experience I'd had contemplating the superior vision of birds of prey, the superior sense of smell of bears and other animals, the ability of so many animals to outrun the fastest humans. It was particularly vision that bothered me the most. I remember saying, "God, why didn't you give people the best vision?" Of course I think we should have the best of everything. I didn't really expect him to answer, but I heard the response, "Yours is good enough." Good enough? I was a little offended. That's not the answer I was expecting! But then I realized how I took it for granted that we humans were what creation was all about—yes, my sense of entitlement. It slowly dawned on me that God created all, rejoicing in all he created, giving each species what they needed, and perhaps blessing humans with an interdependedness that indeed helps us to fulfill our purposes. These were my thoughts as I walked down that long flat Roman road.

I saw the first cornfields I'd seen after so many miles of vineyards and olive groves in Navarre and La Rioja, then miles of closely cut hayfields. The cornstalks here are much shorter than you'd see at home, maybe they aren't hybridized and chemically fertilized. As for fertilizer, I first smelled, and only then did see, truckload after truckload of manure spread out on a field. I saw a tiny aged John Deere tractor and thought of the Little Engine that Could.

We walked into the village of Calzadilla de la Cueza—a big name for a little cowtown. The hotel owner greeted us with overwhelming friendliness and enthusiasm, joking and laughing loudly. The bartender was just as effusive and outgoing, they both seemed eager to make our stay comfortable. We walked up three flights of stairs to our room and then back down to eat a plate of good vegetables—a salad, green beans, and white asparagus. We rested in the afternoon, still struggling to recover.

Supper was in the hotel dining room—cream of vegetable soup with a hearty beef stew and French fries. There was such a good spirit in this place—the owner, another waiter, and the bartender so friendly and eager to help, the owner showing off his Camino tattoos. He had walked it four times. We were in our room by 9:00, and the bar suddenly got very busy and loud—the locals had arrived. But it was quiet by 10:00 and we slept very well.

Calzadilla de la Cueza to Sahagún

reakfast at the hotel—order whatever you want and pay five euros; I smiled at the simplicity. We had coffee, toast, yogurt, and orange juice, and then were off with our headlamps blazing. It was very overcast so it stayed dark longer. We enjoyed a quiet walk on paths through farmlands of plowed fields with dark mountains in the distance. There was a gentle breeze which spoke to me of spirit and presence. Yes, God was there. I heard God in the muted chirping of birds.

We were mostly all alone today but encountered two local women walking mid-morning on the highway carrying buckets and cleaning supplies. Brian was a little ahead of me at the time and they stopped when we met and began talking loud and fast to me—in Spanish. I didn't understand a word but their smiles were bright and friendly. Finally I said, "Okay, *gracias,*" smiled, and went on. Brian was waiting for me, and I told him I didn't have a clue. He told me they just wanted to give me a hard time for walking twenty steps behind my man.

We arrived at the hotel we'd reserved in Sahagun and were a little disappointed to realize the heart of Sahagun was still a kilometer in the distance. This was a big hotel on the outskirts frequented by tour buses, not where we really wanted to stay. But it was a nice place and our room was pleasant. We went downstairs to get something to eat and found the restaurant closed and deserted except for a couple of guys cleaning up after a private tour group had eaten. They told us what time they opened—in three hours. Brian looked at the young man and said, "*Tengo hambre!*" (I'm hungry!) It was kind of pathetic. The guy looked at him and then said "*Ok, un momento.*" He disappeared into the back and came back with two sandwiches. He poured us each a glass of red wine. Bread and wine, the elements of communion. Freely given, as he waved off our offer of payment. We gave thanks and partook.

Later, taking my laundry down to the front desk, I encountered a man in hiking boots limping down the hall. In an effort to be friendly, I said, "*Peregrino?*"

The man replied with a simple "*Sí.*"

To show off my ever increasing language proficiency, I said, "*Ah, tambien,*" which means, "Me too." We got on the elevator together, silent once again.

After a minute, the man ventured forth with "*Hable inglés?*" to which I replied, "*Sí.*"

And then he let it out, as if I was a priest hearing his confession. "Well, I cheated. Just took a bus from Burgos." (That was seven days walking for us.)

I said, "Well, everybody's got to do their own Camino. My husband won't let us cheat," inferring that I wasn't any better than he was, that I might have done the same. "We're carrying all our stuff all the way."

"You walked all the way across that boring Meseta?" he seemed amazed.

"I enjoyed it. It looks like where we're from—the Midwest, in the United States." Wow, did I just say I enjoyed it? Well, I did! Even when I was suffering I dearly loved it and wouldn't have given it up for anything. Even though it had been hard and I'd complained, I was very defensive of the Meseta—it was like a family member being maligned. And if the man cheated, he only cheated himself.

"Well, my hat's off to you," he said, as the elevator door opened.

"Where are you headed now?" I asked.

"I'm walking into town for dinner. You?"

"We're too tired. We're just eating here."

A funny conversation, but there was great truth in the fact that I was cherishing every minute and wouldn't have given any of them up. Oh, there were times when I was tempted, but not really. I enjoyed indulging myself with daydreams of skipping over some parts, the hard parts, but then quickly realizing I didn't want to miss any of it. It would be like wishing a part of your life away. I constantly recognized how much of an allegory for life this walk was. I am so thankful when I look back over my life and am able to see that grace has worked backward redeeming the hard times, infusing them with the beauty that was always there if only I could see it.

That very day I was texting with a friend back home who was going through a very rough time and she told me, "How I long to take a plane ride over this Meseta part of my life!" I know, I know, but not really. We just have to give God time to do the beautiful work of grace. One of the most influential books in my life, first read over thirty years ago, was C.S. Lewis's *The Great Divorce*. This quote was spoken in that great work of fiction by a character named George MacDonald, inspired by Lewis's lifelong literary mentor, George MacDonald.

"Son," he said, "ye cannot in your present state understand eternity...That is what mortals misunderstand. They say of some temporal suffering, 'No future bliss can make up for it,' not knowing that Heaven, once attained, will work backwards and turn even that agony into a glory."

We spent a quiet afternoon and evening at the hotel, staying in our room, going down for a *menú del día* in the restaurant café that night. My cough was slowly getting better, would Brian's blisters ever do the same?

Sahagun to El Burgo Ranero

e were up early and walked fast. I was exhausted and achy, my cold still hanging on. Brian was miserable and a little irritable. It had to be awful to hurt so much for so long, and I felt so bad for him. I had been really proud of how he had tried not to let it get him down. The day off hadn't really seemed to make much of a difference—what else could we do? I was frustrated and worried about him. I was afraid his foot was infected and wanted him to try to see a doctor, which he quickly dismissed. At one point I asked in exasperation if he was just going to keep walking until he fell over in a ditch from blood poisoning. He said he might, and I knew that he's stubborn enough that it could be true. We passed yet another memorial marker to a dead pilgrim—a big gravestone right on the trail. I said sarcastically, "I hope I don't have to buy one of those for you." He shot back, "Don't worry about it, I bet they don't cost as much as you'd think."

We walked all the way into the town where he'd booked a hotel yesterday, passing a big truck stop out on the highway that looked like it was straight out of Nebraska. I was glad we weren't staying there! We walked all the way through the town and couldn't find the hotel, only to finally pull it up on the GPS and realize, yup, it's the truck stop out on the highway. We doubled back, grumbling all the way. We walked past the gas pumps, the big noisy tractor trailers, and on inside to the diner/convenience store. Turns out a truck stop is a truck stop is a truck stop. This one had slot machines and lots of video games and was crowded and noisy. We checked into our room on the second floor, which was clean but colorless. Dingy grey walls with no artwork or decor, non-descript bedding—it was a blah room that matched our blah attitudes. I opened the window to get some air, but what we got were flies, diesel fumes, and the noise of idling trucks.

We went downstairs to the busy dining room and I had a big plate of *arroz negro con calamares*. That's black rice with calamaris, the rice made black with the ink of cuttlefish. It stains your teeth and lips black and is perfect truck stop food if you can't get biscuits and gravy. (Actually, it is pretty tasty.) I spent the afternoon lying on the bed in the stuffy little room without a chair, catching up on Instagram, texting with friends back home, and resting. The dark mood was like a cloud that we couldn't shake. We didn't talk much that afternoon. If I had thought we were in the Slough of Despond before, we were really in it then. I had thought we had dug out but we had only dug deeper in. This might have been the low point of the Camino, the truck stop on the highway outside El Burgo Ranero, almost exactly halfway across the Camino, where we swatted flies in a stuffy room, grumpy and a little bored.

About eight o'clock we went down to the diner. The waitress thought we surely wanted to go into the noisy crowded *comedor* and have a big meal but no, we really just wanted to share a sandwich in the deserted diner. We sat in a booth by the window and she came to take our order. She was exactly what you'd expect a waitress at a truck stop to be, pleasantly plump and gregarious, with a big smile, encouraging our meager attempts at Spanish, complimenting us on how well we spoke! Of course it wasn't true, it was a game; she was just a friendly Spanish waitress in a truck stop, but we found ourselves laughing together with her. And laughter is like medicine; it makes you feel better. I was grateful for this dear woman, another Camino angel. I found my spirits were lighter; the dark mood was lifting. I gazed out the big window through the gas tanks and commented on the hazy sky. The combines had been running all day bringing in the harvest, and the atmosphere was filled with the dust of that harvest. It was a golden corn haze that filled the sky. It looked so much like Nebraska.

We were soon served an enormous grilled ham and cheese sandwich on good Spanish bread, the golden cheese oozing out the sides. It was a truck stop sized sandwich, plenty big to split. It was delicious, just exactly what we wanted. True comfort food.

And then Brian pointed, "Look!" and I turned my head to see the most gorgeous sunset I've ever seen in my life. The sky was alive with color—purple and red and pink and gold—colors of the sun mixing with the harvest dust to create such beauty. I gasped and ran outside to take pictures standing among the gasoline pumps. It was just stunning. I came back inside, took a few more bites, and we watched the sky change, requiring me to run back outside and take more pictures.

Suddenly the whole atmosphere had changed. Instead of despair I felt hope. We shook off the Slough of Despond and ended the day on a much better note. Hopeful.

El Burgo Ranero to Mansilla de las Mulas

Above all, trust in the slow work of God.
We are quite naturally impatient in everything
to reach the end without delay.
We should like to skip the intermediate stages.
We are impatient of being on the way to something

unknown, something new.
And yet it is the law of all progress
that it is made by passing through
Some stages of instability—
and that it may take a very long time.

And so I think it is with you;
your ideas mature gradually—let them grow,
Let them shape themselves, without undue haste.
Don't try to force them on
as though you could be today what time
(that is to say, grace and circumstances
acting on your own good will)
will make of you tomorrow.

Only God could say what this new spirit
gradually forming within you will be.
Give Our Lord the benefit of believing
that his hand is leading you,
And accept the anxiety of feeling yourself
in suspense and incomplete.

This prayer poem by Pierre Teilhard de Chardin, a Jesuit paleontologist and philosopher, was one I meditated on frequently before and during the Camino. Yes, I want to trust in the slow work of God! And this slow Camino is helping me to do that. We have slowed down from our jet-fueled life, from whizzing about in planes and automobiles, from running from appointment to appointment. We have slowed down to Godspeed.

Godspeed. It's an archaic English way of saying goodbye, bon voyage, have a good journey. May God be with you. But what is Godspeed? How fast is God? Is God indeed slow? I remember a conversation we had with Marina so long ago at dinner in Almos de Atapuerca. We wondered about the speed of the Camino, about Godspeed, and the slowness of God. Marina said with wide eyes, "No! God is very fast!" And I suppose God is, when God needs to be. But does God ever need to be?

This transforming work God does in all our lives is only as fast as we let it be. It is hindered only by our inability to yield to it, to accept it, to open to it. How long does it take? As long as it takes. How long does it take to walk the Camino? How long does it take to live a life? If you're lucky, a long, long time.

The walk to Mansilla de las Mulas wasn't particularly memorable but it was enjoyable. We left the truck stop and walked into the town where we found a very welcoming albergue with a breakfast café. (And a trampoline! And a guitar hanging on the wall for *peregrinos* to play—Brian was particularly impressed with that.) "Oh! We could have stayed here," I silently wished but then the realization came that we would have missed the blessings of the truck stop which only continued to grow in meaning as the days went on. Maybe next time. Yes, Brian can play the guitar while I jump on the trampoline. One can only dream!

We walked on. The mountains in the north were more predominant now; we would be crossing them in six days. We walked in a pleasant silence much of the way, and I found myself praying for a lot of different people. I prayed for my 17-year-old niece, Erica, who would be having a very big surgery while we were gone. I hated to not be there but mindfully began praying for her every time I saw a church, which was often. I prayed for my family, for friends at home, for friends around the world. We reached a café near Reliegos and shared a plate of cheese under a weeping willow tree, and soon after that we reached Mansilla de las Mulas. We checked into a *pensión* next door to El Jardín del Camino, the Garden of the Camino. It was a lovely walled garden, part of a restaurant, café, and charcuterie where we whiled away much of the afternoon in absolute splendor. It was a perfect place to sit and read and eat and drink. The sun was shining and the weather was glorious.

I walked to the nearby church by myself, the *Iglesia de Santa Maria*. It was an eighteenth-century church built over the remains of a twelfth-century one. It was empty and quiet except for the piped-in choral music playing, and the atmosphere drew me to prayer. I said my morning liturgy and was awed to hear how my whispered prayers echoed in a church like that. I truly felt like I wasn't the only one praying, that somehow I was joined to the prayers of others. Mansilla de las Mulas left particularly fond memories. It was a good day and a good night. We found ourselves looking forward to tomorrow, when we would enter the big city of Leon, the end of the Meseta.

Mansilla de las Mulas to León

We started early and walked fast, arriving at our hotel in León in only four hours, having walked twelve miles. Brian's feet felt better and I suppose the combination of that and the excitement of being in León was what propelled us forward. We had splurged on a nice hotel in Plaza Mejor Square and arrived to find the city packed and a big festival going on. We walked through huge crowds looking for somewhere to eat, somewhere calm and quiet. We found *La Mary* and had one of the best meals of the Camino—a starter of foie gras and then duck breast for me and oxtail for Brian. It was so good I told him we needed to come back for dinner, especially after I saw risotto on the menu.

There hadn't been anyone in the restaurant when we showed up at 1:45, but it filled up soon after and people were being turned away so I knew we probably needed a reservation. I proudly requested one in Spanish. *"Puede hacer una reservación, por favor, para esta noche?"* I said to the waitress.

"Sí. A que hora?"

I understood! She wanted to know what time! I said, *"Ocho,"* and she countered back with *"Nueve."* But I didn't want to come at 9:00, that was a little too late for pilgrims, and besides, we were going to the pilgrim blessing service at the *Basilica de San Isodoro* at 7:00. So I said again, *"Ocho?"* and she responded with a firm *"Nueve."*

Okay, perhaps there were no open tables at 8:00. I understood that. And so I agreed, "*Nueve*" it was.

We then made our way through the crowded medieval streets of this old city to visit the León Cathedral, considered by many to be the most beautiful cathedral in Spain. The exterior was stunningly magnificent, soaring Gothic towers and turrets, beautiful arches. The white stone stood out brilliantly from the surrounding buildings. But the church closes early on Sundays, and today was a Sunday. It wouldn't open again until 9:30 tomorrow morning.

I desperately wanted to see the inside, and I implored Brian to let us stay over and see it in the morning. He agreed although it would mean we wouldn't get away until 10:00 at the very earliest. (That argument had no impact on me. What could it possibly matter? It's not like we were on a schedule!) And so we spent our afternoon walking the beautiful streets of León, enjoying the crowds and the people, and then went to the Basilica just before the 7:00 pilgrim blessing service. There were a surprising number of people there when we arrived. I understand now it was because it was a Catholic feast day, the Feast of San Froilan, who I learned is the patron saint of León. We took a seat on one of the hard wooden benches and waited for the mass to begin.

An old priest was seated up front, head bowed quietly as he sat in his long black robe. Seven o'clock came and went and he made no move to begin the mass. We continued to wait—7:10, 7:20, as the church continued to fill. I was impatient, aware of how hard the bench was, squirming to find a more comfortable position. I guess it was the fast pace of our morning that made my legs ache so badly. I took some Ibuprofen without any water. A cell phone rang out in the quiet and I was shocked when the priest seated at the altar up front pulled his phone out and began to talk, loudly and animatedly. It was as if he had suddenly sprung to life and it seemed so incongruous. The call lasted less than a minute. He put his phone away, dropped his head, and continued to sit.

Finally, at 7:30, another priest came through a door behind the altar and began the mass. I tried hard to enter into the spirit of the mass, but it's hard when you don't understand the language and besides, we'd been sitting a long time. I was so ready to be done when it was finally concluded around 8:15. It was fortunate I hadn't gotten the 8:00 dinner reservation I'd requested. But at the conclusion, the telephone priest sprung to life again and invited all the pilgrims to come to the front for their blessing. There were at least twenty of us and they handed out prayers to pray in our various languages—Spanish, English, Italian, German, French. This little service was more meaningful to me and the priest who officiated was very passionate about the Camino. He gave us a short sermon, an exhortation in Spanish, some of which I actually understood. I was even more impressed with Brian's comprehension the next day when we encountered another church and he said, "Oh, this is the church the priest told us to be looking for as we walked today."

We finally left the basilica a little after 8:30 and made our way through the crowds of festival celebrators, winding our way to the restaurant once again. We arrived ten minutes early, approached the door, and stopped in our tracks. We looked into a completely dark and empty restaurant.

"It's closed!" I cried out. I was disappointed, yes, that we weren't going to be able to eat there, but maybe even more because I had evidently totally misunderstood the woman with whom I'd made the reservation. I felt confused and frustrated with my lack of language—not just tonight, but the accumulated frustration of the weeks preceding. I turned to walk away but then thought to check the sign posted in the windows, the restaurant's hours. Sure enough, it said that it opened at 9:00. I suddenly understood why we couldn't get a table at 8:00. We sat down on some stairs across the plaza to wait. Promptly at 9:00, the lights were switched on just as two different parties of diners met at the front door from opposite directions. We got up, walked over, and were soon seated.

We had made those reservations because I'd seen risotto on the menu. All day I looked forward to risotto. Why I even looked at the menu might be unclear to some people, but I did so because I am an Enneagram Seven and I wanted to savor all the possibilities. I then saw they had Tagliatelle with Gorgonzola cheese sauce and spinach. Very impulsively, I changed my order, and when it came, it was very good, but not near as special as the risotto that Brian ordered, which was incredible. He let me have a bite and shook his head in disbelief that I had come there expressly for risotto and then changed my mind at the very last minute. I had to remind myself that this was not my last meal and that I was perfectly happy with the pasta. It was funny, but maybe you had to be there. And if I ever get to go back to Leon, I will definitely go to *La Mary* and order the risotto.

Leon to Villadangos del Páramos

We slept in the next morning, had a beautiful breakfast buffet at the hotel, and then hoisted on our packs to go to the cathedral. I would have liked to have left our bags at the hotel so we could enjoy the cathedral unburdened, but since the cathedral was on our way out of town, backtracking wasn't practical.

I had been impressed by the glorious cathedral when we stood outside it yesterday, but the interior was so beautiful that it brought me to tears. It had a very different effect on me than the cathedral in Burgos had. It was achingly beautiful—the stained glass, the statues and paintings, the wood carving—the overall effect intended to bring glory to God. I kept imagining poor serfs from a thousand years ago and the effect it must have had on them. Brian was very moved, too, and we spent forty-five minutes taking it in before we exited and continued walking the crowded city streets of Leon on a sunless day, following the scallop shells and yellow arrows a long time before we finally left the city behind.

We stopped at a tiny café along the highway, sharing our usual *bocadillo jamón,* which sounds so much more elegant than "ham sandwich." The café was decorated with vintage Coca-Cola memorabilia, and as we ate, I took it all in and finally succumbed to the advertising all around me; I went back up to the bar and ordered a Coke Zero *con limón*. Brian laughed at me for being so easily influenced.

Just down the street was the modern church La Virgen del Camino. We approached from the back along one side and would have passed it unawares, except I happened to turn around and noticed the strikingly unusual architecture. We went inside before heading on down the road to the next village.

We found our lodging for the night—once again, a *pensión* connected to a bar popular with the locals. Arriving mid-afternoon, we found the bar full of men playing cards—at least three tables of four with more onlookers than players, some carefully intent upon the play while others seemed to just enjoy the camaraderie. While the waitress worked to check us in, copying info from our passports and looking up our reservation, I watched them and it made me happy to see them together. It was very human and real and certainly beat watching TV alone.

Villadangos del Paramos to Hospital de Orbigo

rian's feet were definitely better! The huge blister that had so plagued him was suddenly almost healed and not causing him pain. We were so grateful and talked about that on the road to Hospital de Orbigo this morning. We'd had three good days of walking, and he remarked on how suddenly things had changed since Mansilla de las Mulas.

Mansilla de las Mulas? It suddenly occurred to me that that was the place I'd sent a photo of his foot to my friend who had prayed for my own foot weeks ago, early on the Camino. I'd been really worried when he took the bandages off that day in Mansilla—the blister looked horrible, like it hadn't healed at all. And now to realize that God and the prayer of a friend thousands of miles away had made a difference made me rejoice and marvel. We were also constantly aware of being held in prayer by our friends and church family back home, like yet another river carrying us along.

Today was our shortest day yet, only seven miles, as we needed to break up a nineteen-mile stretch and were planning twelve miles tomorrow. Ironically, on this shortest day we each developed a new blister, both of which healed quickly and didn't cause any trouble. In fact, we laughed about them!

We landed in a charming place, Hospital de Orbigo, a town famous for one of the longest and best preserved medieval bridges from the thirteenth century. We stayed in a classy little hotel right at the end of this bridge, Don Suero de Quinones. A famous jousting tournament took place here in the year 1434. A knight from Leon, the original Don Suero de Quinones, had been scorned by a woman and in order to regain his honor challenged three hundred different knights to joust, prevailing over all, one after another, over thirty straight days. This story was perhaps an inspiration for Miguel Cervantes writing his epic novel, *Don Quixote*, a few centuries later.

We once again enjoyed a very friendly innkeeper who checked us into our room, got us a small lunch, washed our laundry, and then waited our table in his restaurant that night. This small town with the beautiful bridge left indelible Camino memories.

Hospital de Orbigo to Astorga

The season was changing, it was getting colder. We started out with headlamps and drizzle. The warm days of the Meseta were over and I had a sense of being in the homestretch. I had to keep reminding myself that we still had 180 miles to go. But we had already done 320! The end seemed close.

Towards the end of the Camino, there is a place where all pilgrims symbolically lay down their burdens—the *Cruz de Ferro*, the Iron Cross. It's an important act, something to which a pilgrim is supposed to give much thought. Ideally the burden is something you bring from home, a symbol of what you want to leave behind on the Camino.

I had a small polished black stone I'd been spending some time considering back home. It seemed to represent who I was—it had lots of interesting markings and was mostly polished, with a few rough edges. I have a few rough edges myself. And I liked thinking about all the different things that made me unique, interesting, one of a kind, like nobody else in the entire world. In the weeks before we left for the Camino, I briefly wondered if that stone was what I'd leave behind. Something deep inside pushed back strongly against that idea. No! That stone represented me! I wasn't going to leave "me" behind, but I was eager to quit dragging around anything holding me back, to leave behind the false image of me that kept me from being and seeing what God saw in me when the Trinity of Love joyously created me in their image.

I found another stone, a brightly painted gold stone—smaller, just a pebble really. It seemed to represent my false self, a mask, that candy-coated shell I wear to impress others but mostly to hide from myself. It wasn't real, it was fake, an impostor. It was fool's gold. It spoke to me about a compulsion I struggle with to keep things bright and happy, an inability sometimes to accept things as they are and acknowledge painful realities. I'd brought both stones along and often carried them while I walked, thinking about what they represented. I was going to lay that false self down when I got to the *Cruz de Ferro*, and I was more than ready to do it.

The day remained dark and overcast and the falling mist kept us in our raingear. The sky was grey, the gravel road we walked on was grey, and I felt like we were walking in a black and white photograph. The only colors I saw were the brightly colored packs and rain ponchos on the few pilgrims scattered ahead on the road—dots of red, blue, green, orange. I liked thinking about these pilgrim's journeys and the fact that they too were making progress on the Camino, this great metaphor for life. They were making their own journeys while I was making mine. Our journeys weren't the same, our particular challenges and struggles weren't the same, and I found myself praying for strangers on the Way. I was rejoicing in a big gracious God who never gives up on any of us, but lovingly leads and encourages us to go the distance.

On that grey, colorless day, walking on a rutted gravel road along fields and occasional wooded sections, seeing very few people, I saw a very out-of-place large rock along the side of the road. It stood out in the greyness because it was bright yellow, exactly the color of the small pebble I'd brought from home, my false self. I stopped to examine it a little closer and even lifted one corner up a little bit. Underneath it was just the color of gravel. Someone had spray painted this rock alongside the road. It was very odd, serendipitous, and maybe providential. It was a reminder to me that my little pebble was a phony too, that the color probably didn't go all the way through. I considered finding something to crack my little pebble open with, but I decided I didn't need to be violent with my false self, I just needed to give it up and lay it down. Nevertheless, seeing this rock this day seemed mysterious and significant.

There was also one particular couple, way ahead, that I kept glimpsing throughout the morning. They would disappear around a corner, and then we too would go around that same corner and see them again, way ahead in the distance. One had a long bright orange-red raincape and her companion wore a black one. I imagined them as Much-Afraid with Sorrow and Suffering, the characters in my book. I watched them for a long time; they would stop occasionally, like we do, to take a drink, adjust a pack, or admire the view, but always start up again. I was comforted by the fact that Much-Afraid was on the journey and that I knew she was going to make it, as would I.

We finally crested a hill with a cross at the top and a view of Astorga ahead. There was a man serenading pilgrims with his guitar, singing a fun song about Astorga. We stopped to listen and laugh and put a few coins in his hat. We walked on some distance into the city through the grey drizzle and checked into our hotel, learning it was a national holiday and all the stores and museums were closed. That was disappointing as I'd been looking forward to seeing the Palacio Episcopal designed by the legendary architect, Antoni Gaudi, whose most famous work is the fantastic Sagrada Familia church in Barcelona. Brian had also wanted to buy some sandals here. He now had only one pair of shoes and after a day of hiking, you really need to be able to change and give your feet a break.

At lunch we inquired about the holiday and learned they were celebrating Columbus Day! What? We knew it was Columbus Day back home, but this was Spain! Of course, the voyage of Columbus was financed by Ferdinand and Isabel, the King and Queen of Spain. The "discovery" of the new world was a real boon to Spain, too, as the riches claimed there financed the Spanish Empire, so Columbus Day was a cause for celebration here. Spain became the superpower of the fifteenth and sixteenth centuries, the foremost global power of its time, and was the first to be called "the empire on which the sun never sets." Superpowers come and go, but the kingdom of God, whose power rests in self-sacrificing love rather than conquest, will never cease.

I read that Queen Isabel also traveled to Santiago seeking a cure for childlessness. I seriously doubt if she slept in any bunk beds along the way. Isabel and Ferdinand are also infamous as the instigators of the Spanish Inquisition—witch hunts seeking out infidels and heretics and burning them at the stake, and a tremendous persecution of Jews ending a long period of religious tolerance where Jews, Christians, and Muslims lived together in peace and goodwill. How very sad and tragic this was.

After lunch I told Brian I was going for a walk. He laughed, saying he'd had enough. I was glad it wasn't his feet that kept him at the hotel. I walked through the almost empty city admiring the buildings and store windows. I wanted to see at least the outside of the Palacio Episcopal and was surprised when I got there to find it was open, even though we'd been told it was closed. Gaudi's work is always so original, so surprising, even quirky. Sometimes it's even Dr. Seuss-like, although the palace really is not that. It is light and colorful and spectacular. Next door was the Cathedral, and I visited there too. They had a fascinating museum where I lingered a long time, and when I came out in the late afternoon, the streets were filling with people and the stores were opening.

I was excited; Brian could buy some sandals! I hurried back to the hotel and led him to a sporting goods store I'd found only a block away. I was so excited I tripped over a step at the door to the store and body-slammed onto the sidewalk. I wasn't hurt, just embarrassed. He bought some Keens and was very happy with them the rest of the trip.

He'd had a good afternoon too, and his news for me was that he'd spent the afternoon booking all the accommodations for the rest of the trip. He'd researched and then made phone calls mostly in Spanish. It was nice to have that out of the way. The really good news was that we now knew we wouldn't need our sleeping bags and could mail them on to Santiago tomorrow. I wasn't just symbolically lightening my load, I was literally lightening it. Hooray!

Astorga to Rabanal del Camino

*I*n the morning I painstakingly went through my pack, shoving my sleeping bag and everything I thought I could possibly do without into a plastic sack. It was pathetically little. I was already doing without everything I thought I could possibly do without. But I added my beloved sleeping bag liner, my towel, sunscreen, lotion, and some leaflets I'd collected from places we'd visited. There had been no purchased souvenirs, no t-shirts or trinkets. The box we mailed off with our combined items weighed seven pounds. I couldn't tell my pack was much lighter, but there was definitely more space. I'd been really pleased with the pack I'd bought for the trip; I liked how it was organized and it fit me well. But my hips felt the weight. They ached. My feet still ached, too, but the pain was less than before. It was tolerable, the price for carrying the pack, the price for walking the Camino.

Today was still overcast but dry. As we walked out of the city we found a tiny little church right on the outskirts and felt drawn inside. It was the *Ermita del Ecce Homo*, Valdeviejas, Leon. A man, perhaps the pastor, was inside and welcomed us with a big smile. It was a humble church, a little homespun, but very much a Jesus-centered church. Prayers lined the walls in both Spanish and English. One was the Pilgrim's Prayer:

> *Jesus, my Lord, my friend*
> *You, the icon of God,*
> *You, fountain of Communion, of freedom and love.*
> *You, who are my servant, walk always with me.*

A Jesus church—*Ecce Homo, Ecce Deus*—behold the Man, behold the God. The God Man. There was a small stained glass version of the Trinity Icon, Rublev's Icon, my favorite icon, the icon portraying the divine dance that we are all invited into, the *perichoresis.* Another sign on the wall in Spanish and in English:

> *The journey (camino) is the transformation that happened in the*
> *humanity of Jesus. Now by the Holy Spirit, it can and should happen*
> *in you.*

Those who decorated this church understood the purpose of the Camino. They understood the purpose of life. I had seen great grandeur in the cathedrals of Spain, but I was encouraged and blessed by this humble parish church.

We walked on. We met an American pastor, Ken, and talked together of the many influences we had in common—Richard Rohr, Walter Brueggemann, Stanley Hauerwas, N.T. Wright. We had our late morning *bocadillo* break and walked on to El Ganso where we saw the cowboy bar and got a quick drink en route to Rabanal del Camino. We walked on in the quiet of the afternoon, just the two of us, to a place where the road parallels a path through the woods. I'll always choose the path over the road, even though most of the time the road was just a few yards away. Alongside the path was a fence that passing pilgrims have decorated with hundreds of crosses by weaving twigs into the metal mesh. We were climbing the well-worn path when suddenly, out of nowhere, a terrible pain grabbed my left shin.

It made me yelp and stop. "Ow!" I said, rubbing it. It was a quick, sharp pain and I didn't want to experience it again. We went on a few steps when it hit me again. And then again. And again.

The pain had come out of nowhere with no warning. It felt like my bone was broken, and sharp splinters were poking the insides of my leg. I've had shin splints before, and these were similar but a hundred times worse. And we still had a few miles to go. I began to panic. What was going on? Was I going to make it? I knew I could finish today by sheer willpower, but what about tomorrow? Was our Camino over?

Brian was very sympathetic. He wanted to take my pack, but I refused. The problem wasn't my pack, it was my leg! Besides, my pack was lighter today than it had ever been, and I wanted to carry my own pack the entire way. We did move over and start walking on the road about ten yards away as it was a little smoother. I kept gazing longingly at the path and the fence of crosses. Was I running from my cross? Oh God, I hoped not.

I was moving at a snail's pace now, and it looked like a storm was moving in. I was trying to move faster, but I just couldn't make myself. I kept pushing on, remembering an admonition I'd received that I'd have an opportunity to find God in the pain on the Camino. I found myself musing on how often the Scripture refers to Jesus walking from village to village, exactly what I was doing. I began to imagine him walking with me, right there on my right side, Brian on my left. I talked to him, asked him to heal me, take the pain away, and got no answer. He just continued to walk with me in silence.

It was definitely going to storm; the wind was picking up and the smell of rain was in the air. The first big drops of rain came and we had to stop to put on our raincoats. I was digging in my pack when Brian said, "You know I'm going to take that when you're done with it."

I replied evenly, "If you do, just know you'll be responsible for the first fight we've had on the Camino." Yes, I was testy. My leg hurt. Brian wisely remained silent. He did not take my pack.

We walked on, I continued to ask Jesus to take away the pain, and the pain continued to grip me. Finally, in exasperation, I spoke to Jesus silently in my heart these words, "If you're not going to do something, you're not much good, just walking alongside me. At least Brian has offered to take my pack! Come on—I know you can take away this pain!"

I was brutally honest with Jesus, but it didn't change anything; I was still feeling pain. We walked on another twenty minutes through the village of Rabanal del Camino to get to the *Hosteria el Refugio*. Brian saw the sign and walked ahead fifty yards or so. Fortunately, the threatened rain hadn't materialized; the storm had blown over. I was determined to enjoy the village, thinking this could possibly be the last day of my Camino, and had stopped to take a picture. I looked up and saw him waving me into the *albergue*, so I tried to hurry.

I got to the doorway and realized my leg wasn't hurting.

I turned in, followed Brian and the *hospitalero* up some steps, down some others, a rather circuitous route to get to the check-in desk. My leg wasn't hurting. We checked in and walked up a flight of stairs to our room. My leg still wasn't hurting. But my mind was reeling. I was cautiously wondering if the pain might come back. I didn't go for a walk after we got settled in—not this day! I was filled with a sense of awe, an awareness that God did indeed heal me. And I felt ashamed and embarrassed about my ugly outburst to Jesus—did I really tell him he was no good? Yes, that was what I'd said in my heart, and God knows all that is in my heart.

This experience on the road to Rabanal del Camino was profound. It was mysterious. The pain never came back, and the walk the next day was wonderful. I pondered this prayer experience (what else can I call a conversation with Jesus?) for a long time. I felt bad about my frustration and impatience; I felt guilty for complaining to Jesus. Not that I don't complain on a regular basis, I can whine as well as anyone. But what I said was so....disrespectful? Impertinent? Rude? A display of poor manners?

I wrestled through my feelings about that day and finally acknowledged that what I was most of all in that moment was honest. I read a lot of that kind of honesty in the Psalms, the prayer book of Jesus and the Jewish people. Verses like *"Come on, God, come down here and do something!"* Passion and pathos, genuinely expressed emotion. And I had a distinct impression that as I said those words to the Man Jesus walking with me on the road, he didn't react. Not at all. Not angrily or with hurt feelings. He just listened to me, let me verbalize my frustration, let me lament. He also healed me. In his own time. At the right time. And not right when I demanded him to.

I was reminded of Martha's lament to Jesus at the death of her brother Lazarus—*"Jesus, if you'd been here my brother would not have died!"* I like to think that the tone of her outburst was similar to mine, and I moved from feeling guilty to feeling surprisingly closer to God as a result. I'm grateful now for the experience and grateful for the pain that brought about the experience. It's hard for me to be grateful for pain, but I'm growing into that place and am ironically grateful that I'm grateful.

We liked the *albergue* a lot. The café downstairs was cozy and inviting; the evening had turned cold. We went to a Vespers service at a monastery adjacent to the albergue. It was a new community of Benedictine monks who had come from Germany and revitalized an old deconsecrated church. There was an incredible beauty in the thought of that—a church which had died, been buried, but brought back to resurrection life. The Pascal mystery.

The church was small but full of pilgrims; the mass was done in several languages—English, Spanish, Latin, and an Asian language, maybe others. Part of it was chanted, which was moving and something we hadn't heard much. The church building itself was special. When a church is deconsecrated, the decorations are removed, and now this one had been redecorated very simply. Unlike many of the churches we'd seen in Spain, Jesus was the central focus, a simple but beautiful crucifix at the front. We were all invited to come forward to receive the Eucharist. It was a wonderfully meaningful service.

Afterwards, we had dinner at the *albergue*. The American pastor, Ken, and a Peruvian American woman joined us. We talked about the phenomenon of Christian pilgrimage, of Scotland, Iona, and St. Andrews. It was a rich and enjoyable evening as well as a rich and enjoyable meal. I had pumpkin carrot soup and cod. I went to bed that night marveling over God's goodness and grace, my experience on the road, and also the strange painted stone I'd seen that morning. Tomorrow was the day I would leave my little false self painted stone behind.

Rabanal del Camino to El Acebo

I woke up feeling great, with no pain at all in my leg. It had gone as suddenly and mysteriously as it came. I was overcome with gratitude and also thankful for the fact that Brian's feet were well and that we were finishing the Camino relatively pain-free together! Today's weather was dry but surprisingly cold and windy. We stopped soon to put on our raincoats just for some extra protection from the wind and felt sorry for people we saw going by in shorts. The wind kept up, and we eventually put on everything we had including gloves and stocking caps. I was wearing my long sleeve T-shirt, a fleece, a down jacket, and my raincoat, and was still freezing. We were going up, up, up ever since leaving Astorga yesterday, to over four thousand feet in elevation.

We finally reached the miniscule village of Foncebadón and ducked into a tiny packed café where a fire was blazing in the fireplace and hot drinks and snacks were available. Again, the sense that Camino angels were present everywhere providing all we needed. On the crowded mantle was a Rumi poem which greatly speaks to me:

> *Come, Come, whoever you are—*
> *Wanderer, worshiper, lover of leaving*
> *Ours is not a caravan of despair*
> *Even if you have broken your vow one thousand times—*
> *Come, yet again, come.*

This is the invitation God has for us all. God never gives up on us, never quits loving us, never quits arranging circumstances to draw us in. Even if we have failed a hundred thousand times, the gates will never be shut.

We drank some tea and absorbed the heat of the fire and then stepped back out into the cold, grateful and warmed through. I was reminded of the experience weeks ago hearing *"Come unto me, all you who are weary and heavy laden, and I will give you rest,"* in the Jesus meditation service we'd attended in the Dutch *albergue* at Villamayor de Monjardin, and the realization that Jesus is like the kind host caring for all our needs but never intending for us to camp indefinitely. He calls us to rest so that we can stay on the journey. It made me smile and I walked with joy and a warmed heart all the way to the Cruz de Ferro.

The Cruz de Ferro was a bit anti-climactic. People were clowning around and posing for silly pictures. It wasn't an environment for a protracted and deeply-felt ceremony of laying down our burdens. I didn't want to try to manufacture an emotional experience, and besides, it was cold and we wanted to keep moving.

But I had trouble letting go of my little yellow stone. Yes, it represented my false self, but I found myself wanting to respect it, to care for it tenderly. I didn't want to just throw it down. I ended up finding a scallop shell that someone had left, turned it over, and placed my little bright happy-clappy stone carefully inside. "Goodbye, false self, I no longer need you." I walked away but found myself turning around for one last look.

Brian showed me his heavy black stone before he put it down. It was weighty and substantial and I had to remind myself that it wasn't mine. I have felt his burden many times, but it's not mine and besides, it's been laid down. I prayed to remember that. We walked on. It was bitter cold and a little foggy.

A few miles later, we came upon a food truck, split a sandwich and a delicious cup of chicken broth. As we walked on the sun came out, the fog lifted, and it warmed up just a bit. We were going downhill now and arrived in the picturesque mountain village of El Acebo around 2:00 where we checked into a *casa rural* where we had a reservation. A pleasant man answered the door and welcomed us into his living room where he was ironing towels. Yes, ironing bath towels! I learned ironing towels that have been hung on a clothesline softens them and makes them feel as if they've been in an electric dryer. It was a nice touch.

The man and his wife live in the mountain village and feel very fortunate to live there, grateful that renting out the two bedrooms upstairs to *peregrinos* allows them to do so. A very old man, no doubt the father of one of them, dozed in an armchair. After a shower, we went out to find something more substantial to eat. The sun was still shining, but I wore both jackets and ate outside because it was too beautiful not to. I had a starter of gazpacho and asked if perhaps they could make it *"caliente."* It was just so cold outside and in my mind cold gazpacho warms up to tomato soup. The girl laughed as if shocked and said no one had ever asked for that before. When it came, it was only lukewarm, but it was delicious lukewarm gazpacho. I had a steak and Brian had rabbit, which he raved on, saying it was his best meal yet. I had taken a vow never to eat rabbit again after my horrible dream and was quite happy with steak. We met our host's wife that evening going out, and she insisted Brian wear a heavy wool scarf which she wrapped around his neck herself! El Acebo was a quiet, peaceful stop in a beautiful place. It had been another perfect day on the Camino.

El Acebo to Ponferrada

The next day's walk was down the mountain, partly on a road, partly on mountain trails. A local bike club came pedaling up the steep mountain path we were walking down. We had our *bocadillo* break in Molinseca. Brian saw a carafe of what he thought was olive oil on the bar and tried to put some on his sandwich. The woman tending bar cried out, "No, no!" It turns out that it was actually grapa, a very stout brandy made from discarded grape seeds. That would have been interesting on his sandwich!

Weeks ago mutual friends had made us aware of a woman also on the Camino—these friends hoped very much we would meet one another. It was very unlikely as she was several days behind.

But as we lingered over a longer than usual *bocadillo* break this woman, Lisa, who I recognized from her social media photo, walked up to our table and said, "Well, hello."

I wasn't at all surprised. I had felt like we probably would meet, unlikely as it was. The Camino was consistent in providing just what was needed, and I had a sense of once again just submitting to the flow of the river. She said she had known we would meet too. She had bussed ahead several days due to a scheduling need, having no idea where we were. It turned out we had a lot of mutual friends and very similar spiritual histories and journeys. We visited for a while and realized we were planning on staying in the same city that night, Ponferrada, so we made plans to have dinner together. She sat down to have a break and we hit the trail.

We walked for a long time around the big city of Ponferrada, on the outskirts, and when it seemed we would almost pass it, the path turned inward and we entered the heart of the old city. We finally came to a huge castle, a very impressive edifice, the Castillo de Templars. I would have liked to have gone inside, but we were tired, and the hostel we had reserved was still a long ways off. We walked on past the historic part of the city to an industrial area and finally found it. We had laundry to wash and found a tiny Laundromat nearby with three washers, three dryers, and four chairs, and sat together waiting on our laundry. It was 5:00 when we finished and we were hungry. We texted Lisa and she was ready to eat, too, so we walked a kilometer back to the historic area to meet her only to learn there wasn't any food to be had until 7:00. We ordered some snacks and drinks and had three great hours of conversation, ordering a meal when it was finally available. We talked about Jesus, the church, theology, the enneagram, spiral dynamics, and a thousand other things. It was amazing how much we had in common, how quickly we became fast friends, and how the evening flew by.

For some reason in the night I woke up thinking about what I don't like about who I am. I smiled in the darkness, deciding to accept it all with gentleness and compassion, and went right back to sleep.

Ponferrada to Cacabelos

We left Ponferrada in the mist. We had looked forward to breakfast at a café right outside our hostel as it advertised "*desayuno inglés*"—English breakfast! But we found the café closed at 8:30 in the morning, probably because it was Sunday, something we hadn't factored in. So it was toast, orange juice, and coffee once again. I ate more bread on the Camino de Santiago than I eat in two years at home. Bread is so delicious.

As we left the big city of sixty-two thousand, we passed an enormous church. It was Sunday morning and the church was closed, deserted. It was no doubt another decommissioned church and that made me sad. But a short time later we entered a small village and passed a church where a service was in progress. There was a woman standing out in the road inviting pilgrims inside, telling them they could get their *credenciales* stamped there. It was a very effective outreach strategy because pilgrim packs were lining the exterior. The church door was open wide, and we joined others inside just in time to partake of the Eucharist. What an unexpected treat that was!

We walked on to Cacabelos, another quintessential Camino village with lots of character, and checked into our hotel, dropping off our packs and going straight to the restaurant next door the girl at the hotel had recommended. Shortly after we were seated, it filled up, not with *peregrinos* but locals, families there to enjoy a big Sunday dinner.

We were seated by an enormous open fireplace that was so enjoyable because the air was cool and damp; we ordered the specialty of the house, *arroz con bogavante*, paella with lobster. Our starter was *pastel con salsa rosa*, some kind of paté with crackers. It was all incredibly good, and I ate so much I went to the room, crawled into bed, and didn't leave again until morning.

I finished *Hinds Feet on High Places* and pondered the beautiful ending for a long time. I too was on a pilgrimage and inspired to finish as well as Much-Afraid had, taking heart not in the strength of my abilities but in God who has so gently led me. My Camino was a continued metaphor for this journey through life.

Cacabelos to Trabadelo

We left in the dark and had a pleasant morning's walk amidst clouds and silence, arriving in Villafranca del Bierzo in time for lunch. Villafranca is a popular tourist town, considered one of the most beautiful on the Camino with a romantic castle and an eleventh-century Romanesque church with a famous *puerto de perdón*—a door where absolution could once be obtained for those too sick or weak to continue on to Santiago. Fortunately that doesn't apply to us today! We had a nice lunch in a beautiful plaza and continued through the city. I had read about an alternate route that goes up into the mountains starting on the way out of Villafranca. Back home in America that had seemed appealing but after four hundred miles of walking across Spain, it was not even a consideration. A chance to add two kilometers and lots of elevation gain and loss to our day? No, thanks! When we came to the turn-off, a small cat sat in the middle of the road, and I laughed imagined him telling us, "Thou shall not pass," in a deep Gandalf-ish voice.

We didn't see the sun at all this day, walking mostly on deserted roads, often crossing under high bridges with the modern super highway way above us. It felt like we were walking in an earlier time period on roads that had been forgotten. We reached the tiny quiet village of Trabadelo in the late afternoon and checked into a hostel.

It was definitely getting colder; the season was changing and the air was damp. Our room was cold, the floor was cold, and everything I touched was cold. After showering I was even colder with no way to dry my hair. I got under the covers and shivered, unable to get warm. It was exasperating to see the radiator in the room with no way to turn it on. I finally decided to go downstairs and ask the woman in the café if we could have some heat. I practiced my sentence. *"Habitación es muy frio."*

I wasn't sure if that was the correct way to say the room was very cold, but the woman said, *"Oh, sí!"*—quickly going into a back room. She came back out and said, "Okay!" I assumed she had turned the heat up, said *"Gracias,"* and happily went back to my room. An hour later there was no change. I'm not sure what that was all about.

That night we went across the street to a restaurant offering a *menú del dia*. I was thrilled to get a starter of *judias verdes*—green beans! Yes, a big plate of green beans and they were so delicious. Then a *churrasco* plate—pork, veal, sausages with special sauces and fries. Another hearty meal.

When we got back to the room around 8:30, the radiator was on and the room was warm and dry. I was so thankful for the warmth and for the good meal which had also warmed my heart. I went to sleep aware that the end of the Camino was close.

I remembered imagining before we ever started what I might be thinking about this time. I had worried that I might be longing for the Camino to end and then, when it did, how sad I would suddenly be. Those emotions were ones I was so familiar with. But somehow I had escaped those thoughts. I was living in the moment probably better than I ever had in my life. I wasn't trapped in fears for the future and regrets about the past. I wasn't longing for it to be over; I was loving the present and calm and relaxed about the future, about the Camino ending. I was "loving what is" and it felt great.

Trabadelo to O Cebreiro

We entered into Galicia on this day, the last province. This northwest corner of Spain is a very different area both culturally and geographically. A thousand years ago Celtic people from Ireland arrived on the shores of Iberia, and their influence is still strongly felt. The restaurant last night had Irish music playing, and the walls were decorated with Celtic symbols. It's always damp and frequently raining in Galicia, just like Ireland. But this day we had some very welcome sunshine.

We walked on flat roads until lunchtime and then started going up, up, up—a very steep climb. The map showed three villages about equally spaced—La Faba, Laguna de Castilla, and finally O Cebreiro. Three hard pushes for the afternoon.

La Faba was the first village. It seemed to be a place out of time. There were a few villagers out and about, mainly old people quietly going about their business. A very old woman was stooped over digging dandelions. She had a sack full and when she stood up she was still stooped over. She made me think of the woman in the Bible who was "stooped double and could not straighten up at all," a woman Jesus healed. This woman walked away in that posture no doubt to cook herself a nice pot of greens. I said a silent prayer for her. We left La Faba and continued up the steep path.

Fortunately, I was distracted from the exertion by the beauty of the trail which seemed to become more beautiful the higher we went. We were walking through dark woods on a trail of stone, a trail that was hollowed out by the millions of footsteps that had trod it over the centuries. The ruins of ancient stone walls along the trail were covered in lush green moss, trees covered with ivy and vines. The silence of the woods was captivating; the woods seemed to be enchanted. We walked the trail in solitude, but I felt very distinctly that we were not alone. I sensed others, the spirits of others, those who had gone before us. No, we were not alone.

Who walked on these stones up this steep hill all those years before me? Did they hear the birds singing in the trees as I did, and was there moss growing on the stone walls even then? What blessings did they hope to receive through their pilgrimage to Santiago? I thought about the mysterious phrase in the Apostles Creed—"the communion of saints." Yes! This was that. I was in communion with these saints; they weren't so far away but right here with me. They were the "cloud of witnesses" the Bible talks about and how deeply I sensed their presence. I marveled and worshiped as I walked.

I also thought about the "little people" of Irish lore—the fairies who lived in the woods. Maybe there was a connection; maybe this sense of "someone there" had given rise to the stories of sightings, to the myths and stories that so enrich that culture. It wouldn't be hard to imagine; it wouldn't be hard to believe. Magical, such a sense of the holy.

Up and up and up, and the air was getting cooler. We finally arrived at O Cebriero and I found myself gasping with delight. It was another world, a hobbit hamlet, or maybe a life-size fairy kingdom, a charming quaint stone village filled with stone huts with thatched roofs. O Cebriero was draped in a dense fog increasing the aura of mystery and enchantment.

The tavern where we checked into our rooming house looked like something out of Lord of the Rings; we'd return here later for dinner. Our room was in a beautiful large two-story stone home that had probably belonged to a wealthy family. It had been converted into a rooming house and decorated in Victorian style. Our little room on the second floor had a ruffled purple bedspread and the walls were painted a deep green. On the main floor was a charmingly appealing Old World sitting room with a big fireplace—what a shame I hadn't any time to sit there! I found myself lamenting I couldn't have sat there on "truck stop" day, and I had to remind myself once again that that day had had its own unique blessings! I resolved once again to continue to renew my mind to "love what is"—to embrace each day as it is given to me, to free myself from the trap of living in regret of the past and fear of the future instead of the present moment which is the only time we can actually live.

We walked around the village which was at the top of a large ridge with panoramic views all around, visited the church, attended the nightly pilgrim mass then went to supper. The tavern was packed, and we were lucky to get a table as some others were leaving. Shortly after we sat down, two Germans approached and asked to join us. They introduced themselves as Marc and Rudy. They hadn't known each other before the Camino but had become friends along the way. Rudy said he'd walked from Munich and that it had taken him three months. From Munich south to France, all the way across France, and now all the way across Spain.

We'd been looking forward to the advertised stew simmering on the big stove, but when the waitress took our order she said it was *complet*. So I had a salad and the traditional Galician cabbage soup, and Brian ordered the extremely popular dish—*pulpo*, or octopus. I can eat almost anything, but I draw the line at octopus —rubbery chopped tentacles with obvious "suction cups." (Okay, rabbits are also across the line.) We had some local cheese with honey for dessert. We dearly loved O Cebreiro.

O Cebreiro to Triacastela

*I*t was such a beautiful walk out in the morning shortly before sunrise, walking along the ridge in the scattered mist. The views on both sides were spectacular. I rejoiced in all that was around me; it was a great day. We finally began to descend and it was downhill all the way to Triacastela. Triacastela was a bigger village and we had some trouble finding the *pensión*. The middle-aged woman who checked us in seemed rather bored. Of course she didn't understand a word of English so I guess the interaction with me really wasn't too interesting despite my efforts to be winsome and engaging. She showed us to our room, and after showering, I went to ask about getting some laundry done. I had seen a clothesline from our window.

"*Lavandería?*" I was a little confused over whether to accent the third or the fourth syllable. And yes, it makes a huge difference. But she seemed to understand. And with some pantomime and struggling to understand her Spanish responses, I finally understood I could bring it down to her. Good, I wouldn't have to do it myself. But I guessed she might have to hang it out on the line and it was already mid-afternoon. So I struggled to ask her when I might get it back.

"*Mañana? Ocho?*" (Tomorrow by eight?)

"*No, nueve.*" Oh. That wasn't good. We would want to be gone no later than eight. I decided to negotiate. "*Ocho?*"

We went back and forth a couple of times. I was trying to be charming, but it wasn't doing me much good. The woman never smiled back. She just looked thoroughly bored and slightly disgusted to be talking to such a stupid person. Finally she put her hand up as if to stop me and pointed at a woman I presumed was her sister, the only other person in the café. She was sitting at a table hunched over a newspaper. Without a word, she scraped her chair back, stood up, walked across the room, and disappeared behind a door. I just stood there wondering what was going on. She came back a minute later with a teenage boy who had been called upon to translate. Wonderful, someone who speaks English.

He came and stood beside his mother who was going to do my laundry. So I explained that I needed to have it back by tomorrow morning at eight. He took a deep breath before he said nine. I said that I really needed it by eight. He took another deep breath and said, "Okay."

We had a deal. I said, "Okay, I'll be right back!" intending to go upstairs and get my laundry. I then daringly asked if perhaps she had a laundry basket. I also pantomimed it. I am terrible at charades but desperate times call for desperate measures. She seemed to understand and indicated she would come with me. Wonderful.

We walked upstairs. She opened a door at the end of the hall and came back with a laundry basket. We walked together to our room, I stuffed all our dirty laundry in it, and she walked down the hall and put it directly in a washing machine. This was a fabulous development in our relationship. I said, *"Muchas gracias!"* with *muchas* enthusiasm. The woman just nodded, deadpan.

We walked down the street to a charming restaurant, sat out in the sunshine and ate a big pilgrim meal at 5:00, a delicious seafood soup (*sopa de marisco*) and then steak. Again I was so aware and grateful for the gift that a good meal is—not just fuel for the body but soul-enriching. Shortly after returning to our room there was a knock on the door. There stood the woman who'd done my laundry with the basketful of clean clothes. Gloriously clean clothes I wanted to touch and smell. And at 7:30, not 8:00. 7:30 in the evening, not the morning! Had I not said *"Ocho en la mañana"* repeatedly? *La mañana.* It means in the morning. Tomorrow morning, right? I was so confused. And she hadn't hung it out, as others had—she had a dryer as well as that clothesline. I was about to give up on trying to understand Spanish. If I have any regrets about the Camino, it's wishing I'd worked harder to learn some Spanish before going. But I have to continually remind myself that if I'd known Spanish, I'd have a different story. This is my story, my Camino, and not knowing the language made it what it is. And it's just fine the way it is. Accept it. Embrace it.

The next morning, while eating breakfast in the quiet bar tended by the same woman, a local guy came in who seemed to know her well. He brought her the newspaper and launched into a long story (in Spanish, of course.) I watched the two of them—he went on and on and she just looked at him with the same bored expression she'd given me. I laughed a little to myself, once again reminding myself not to take everything so personally, realizing how hard I had worked trying to make her "like" me. How silly I felt!

Tricastela to Sarria

W e had two routes to choose from today, a longer route that led to an famous monastery or a shorter one that bypassed it. We chose the shorter route and I once again found myself facing that tendency I have to "want it all," worrying about what I might have missed. It's the Enneagram Type Seven passion of gluttony, gluttony for experiences. But the walk was pleasant and I consoled myself with the fact that I could just have easily missed it! In the evening we met our new friend Lisa for a fun dinner. While we waited for her to arrive, Brian picked up the pink guitar that hung outside the restaurant and had "Play me" painted across the front. He sang one Dylan song after another. We were now one hundred kilometers, just sixty-two miles, from the end of the Camino, the last place for people to join and still be eligible to get a Compostella certificate in Santiago. We both felt strong and healthy. Our feet had now accommodated themselves to the walking. I couldn't keep from thinking about hinds' feet—the book and the scripture reference found both in Psalm 18 and Habakkuk 3.

"He shall make my feet like hinds' feet, and set me securely on the high places." Another translation talks about God "enabling me to negotiate the rugged terrain." I remembered the first time I hiked the Longs Peak trail in Rocky Mountain National Park to the Keyhole—six miles one way on a tough trail up four thousand feet after starting at nine thousand. That was the hardest hike I'd ever done at that time and I remember watching a herd of elk from a long ways off as I climbed, drawing closer and closer to them until they suddenly noticed me and ran off. I marveled at the ease in which they negotiated the terrain and lamented that I couldn't do the same.

But God's promise was that he would transform me and enable me to do what had previously been impossible. Yes, I'd since climbed that trail to the Keyhole more than once and it had gotten easier. I'd gone on to do even harder things. I had now walked over four hundred miles across Spain, marvel of marvels, and was confident that soon I'd finish the Camino. But the Camino was a metaphor for my life, the best metaphor I'd ever experienced. I realized with great joy that God's grace was transforming me so that I could do the things I had previously thought impossible. The Amplified Bible translation of this scripture is beautiful: *"The Lord God is my Strength, my personal bravery, and my invincible army; He makes my feet like hinds' feet and will make me to walk, not to stand still in terror, but to walk, and make spiritual progress upon my high places of trouble, suffering, or responsibility!"* This gives me joy—joy inexpressible and full of glory!

Sarria to Portomarín

S arria had been fun. And funny. We had checked into a little hotel on the edge of town and our room, while small, had a fancy shower with all kinds of settings and jets. All I really wanted was a shower and I struggled for five minutes trying to figure out how to turn it on! This is not unusual. I frequently have trouble with mechanical things, as my family well knows. I try not to let it frustrate me, but it makes me feel stupid, and I hate to admit when I can't do simple things like turn on a shower. Finally, in exasperation, I asked Brian to come in and turn on the stupid shower for me. (Yes, it's easier to project the idea of stupidity on the object rather than on myself.) But he couldn't get it to come on either!

That made me feel a little better about myself. I put my sweaty clothes back on, went downstairs, stood at the bar, and waited for the very busy guy who had just checked us in to finish making a *café con leche*. I simply told him, "*No agua*."

He looked at me in confusion. "*No agua?*" And then he understood, his eyes got wide, and he said with a panic, "*No agua!*" He did remind me just a bit of Manuel on *Fawlty Towers*.

He got on the phone, was speaking Spanish rapidly, and I don't know how I understood (but I did!) that they had been working on something, it was out on our entire floor, but that he thought he could get it going again. Something had been forgotten. He sent a woman up to the fourth floor with me; we went in another room; she stuck her head around a corner for a couple of minutes. She did something and indicated that all was well now. Or she guessed it was. And I went back to the room and took a shower.

Another funny thing happened in the morning when we went to check out. We stood at the counter and ordered our normal breakfast of coffee and toast because nothing else was available. I am a big believer in protein for breakfast but rarely was that available on the Camino. We waited for it to be prepared, but then there was nowhere to sit as the two tiny tables were both taken. I noticed an empty dining area down behind the café and asked (with my usual pantomime and cave man language) if it was okay to take our toast and coffee back there. "*Sí*," we were told.

We carried our plates back only to find a huge breakfast buffet all laid out—fruit and cheese and sausages and pastries and even eggs! I went back out front and inquired—it was for us! Included with our room! We didn't know. But you can be sure we took advantage of it and had a big breakfast feast.

I waited outside on the sidewalk while Brian finished up with some packing and visited again with an American man we had run into a couple of times hiking with two other American buddies. His wife had flown in just yesterday and was joining him to hike the last sixty miles. He was waiting for her to come out, too, and was grumbling that even though he'd started in St. Jean and this was her first day, she'd felt inclined to tell him this morning what he needed to do to avoid blisters. I laughed, understanding how irritating that could be and hoping they'd do okay together the remaining days.

I remembered wondering how Brian and I would do together all day every day on our Camino, and I was so thrilled that we hadn't had any squabbles at all—absolutely none! This probably qualified as a Camino miracle. There was that time when I had the terrible pain in my leg, and he threatened to take my pack from me and carry it himself, (what a bad guy!) but I'd warned him that he'd be responsible for starting a fight. We'd talked before coming about avoiding conflict. I told him the thing that would really set me off was being hurried, specifically him tapping his watch and giving me "that look." I had suggested he might want to consider leaving his watch at home, and he'd said there was no sin in wanting to know what time it was.

And what irritating trait of mine did he bring up? Well, as I recall—none. I am fairly sure though that this doesn't mean I don't have any. So is he a super-tolerant saint? Hmm, I'm not sure what conclusion I should draw. Lord have mercy.

We soon encountered Mark, the German who we'd met in O Cebreiro. We told him we'd run into Rudy last night, suffering from a painful Achilles tendon and spending another night in Sarria. He and Mark hadn't seen one another since Tricastela; Mark said Rudy was religious and wanted to go the long route to visit the monastery in Samos because of the special blessing the monks give there. Rudy had told us at dinner in O Cebreiro that he was Catholic. I'd responded that I thought Luther had got all the Catholics in Germany. He laughed and said, "No, only about half!"

We walked with Mark a long time that day. Mark said something about how we shouldn't expect miracles on the Camino. I had been thinking that everything on the Camino was a miracle! The beauty of the created world, the people we encountered, the amazing way all our stories were unfolding. We talked about the end of the Camino. I mentioned how fun I thought it would be to sit and watch people finish, watch them come into Santiago. I had a perception of how that would be—in my mind we would stumble out of the woods and suddenly encounter the huge cathedral, which was nothing like what actually happened! Mark felt strongly that it would be wrong to watch people come into Santiago—it would be so emotional and personal. I considered that aspect too and wondered again how I would feel when that day came. Would I be happy? Would I be sad it was over? Mostly now I just felt very peaceful and content. I felt good.

After a while I let Brian and Mark go on ahead talking together and I followed behind, just enjoying being. Enjoying walking, enjoying being alive. Enjoying the sunshine, the cool air, and the goodness of creation.

We saw a sign indicating we were almost to Portomarin, our day's destination. Then a sign indicating that a detour was recommended because the next portion was extremely difficult—to take the bike route which is four tenths of a mile longer. Of course we took the original route, which became a steep and rocky canyon, but we didn't mind it.

Portomarin is a town that was completely moved in the twentieth century due to flooding from a dam, but the city has origins dating back to the tenth century, and many ancient buildings were moved and rebuilt stone by stone. We entered the city by crossing an extremely long bridge I was nervous to walk across, triggering my fear of heights as we looked down over the ruins of the previous city. The ruins looked ancient even though the city had been there only fifty years ago. All that remained were stones. After the bridge we climbed an enormous flight of stairs. It had been a long day—fourteen miles with my still heavy pack. We napped and then enjoyed sitting on the hotel balcony looking over that deep valley, reading and relaxing.

Portomarín to Hospital de la Cruz

e left the city crossing back to the other side on a different bridge. It was foggy, dark, misty. I felt myself craving color. I saw only a bit of blue sky for a short time that day. We were walking only seven miles that day, the only way we could avoid an excessively long day. The trail was definitely more crowded with newcomers and you could always spot them wearing bright crisp new clothes, often in large, loud groups. I tried not to resent the newcomers and to honor their Caminos as their Caminos. At lunch there were eight women in line in front of me for one bathroom. This was not what I was accustomed to.

We reached our lodging by noon and checked into a tiny room, but I soon realized there was no comfortable place to sit. It was raining intermittently which ruled out sitting outside and the only seating in the restaurant was on picnic benches. That left us in our room, which was freezing cold. It was so cold I hated to wash my hair because there was no way to dry it. I looked up the Spanish word for hairdryer on my phone—*secadora*, asked the woman at the restaurant, and she kindly found one for me.

It was a tiny room with a tiny bed, and after I dried my hair I crawled into bed to get warm. There were two huge thick wool blankets in the room in addition to the bedding already on the bed and I piled them on me. They were so heavy that they hurt my tender toes, and I still had trouble getting warm.

This day was a little frustrating. The loud and incessant chatter of the newcomers on the Camino that day had created an atmosphere that was not as peaceful and enjoyable as past days. Going such a short distance made for a very long afternoon. And there was nowhere to be comfortable. We were feeling the pull of Santiago, ready to be there. Would we ever arrive?

We met two American women that night, Pat and Betsy. They weren't together but each hiking alone. They both said they were having trouble and were moving really slowly. Betsy seemed to be at peace with it, but I could tell Pat was very bothered. She knew so much about the Camino, had researched it thoroughly, but the actual walking was much tougher than she'd expected. I was genuinely sympathetic. Pat seemed so disappointed in herself. We tried to be encouraging to both of them.

When we got back to our room, the heat had been turned on. Glory be to God.

Hospital de la Cruz to Palas de Rei

We left in the early morning out into rain. By midmorning it was still darkly overcast. It had been days since I'd seen the sun, and I desperately missed it. We ran into Pat, and I walked and talked with her as Brian went on ahead. We did this often as he'd walked with Mark yesterday and I'd dawdled behind. The difference when I'm walking with someone else is that he's not dawdling behind but suddenly has license to walk fast and get way ahead. I'm aware I should be very grateful he was so patient day after day and slowed down his preferred pace to match mine.

Then Pat said she needed a break and I went on. I was out on a country road all by myself and thoroughly enjoying it, wondering what had happened to all those newcomers from yesterday. Then I heard gunshots—a brand new experience on the Camino. Europeans do not have guns like Americans have guns. I saw a man up on a ridge with a rifle and for just a minute my heart raced, but then I realized he had some dogs with him, a couple of small terriers—birddogs. He was a hunter, wearing an orange vest. (Yikes, I did not have an orange vest!) But I watched the birddogs run to and fro, doing what birddogs do. They were obviously well-trained.

I passed by an old man in a small village who encouraged me to check out a nearby albergue. I told him, "*No necesito albergue. No hablo espanol.*" I gave him a big smile. He seemed to understand.

After a while I saw a patch of blue over the mountains in the horizon and within fifteen minutes the glorious sun reappeared, bringing back the colors. I was so tired of grey and now the yellow sun shone from the blue sky on a green field where vibrant black and white cows grazed. It was startlingly beautiful, as if I'd never seen colors before. I stared, trying to absorb them into my being.

An hour later, a cold wind blew in. It clouded up and began to rain again. I saw a grumpy woman I'd last seen weeks ago; she was still walking. What was her story? I said a prayer for her and for all the unknown stories of those walking the Camino with me.

Brian and I had met up for our *bocadillo* break and walked together on into Palas de Rei, which means Palace of the King. The palace no longer exists, but the name remains. We had a room reserved in a *pensión*, checked in, and showered. The water turned ice cold mid-shower and then the towel bar fell off the wall, but the room was clean and dry and warm which seemed like a great luxury. It was really cold outside. We absolutely had to do laundry today and were nervous about doing it by hand as we were doubtful it would dry by morning.

Our room was a five-minute walk from where we'd checked in and so we walked back carrying our laundry. We'd forgotten to ask about it, but some other pilgrims staying there assured us that was the procedure. We walked back only to be told there were no laundry services on Sunday. She suggested another place where we walked, only to be told that no, not here, perhaps this other place. We inquired at four different places and a kind *hospitalero* working at an *albergue* let us use their washing machine and dryer. But the dryer was small and slow, so the laundry took our entire afternoon. While the clothes washed and dried, we sat in the tiny lobby and enjoyed a snack of fried calamaris the very helpful and caring *albergue* worker cooked up for us. She was another Camino angel, all smiles and love.

As we'd walked around the city looking for a place to do our laundry, I'd spotted Pat getting out of a taxi. I sensed her shame in the way she kept her head down and didn't look around. I didn't let her know I'd seen her and prayed for her. I wanted her to feel good about her Camino even if she hadn't been able to walk the entire way. I'm sure I prayed for other pilgrims every single day— it was just a natural thing to do.

That night we found an especially good pilgrim menu and had chicken with brandy and mushrooms, a salad, wine, and custard for dessert. All for eleven euros which never ceases to amaze me. As the waiter started to walk away I added, "Oh yes, we need some water, too." He turned and said, "It's going to be extra for that!" Ha, that is hysterical. Yes, we'll pay extra for the water. The food was fabulous.

Palas de Rei to Melide

Eggs again for breakfast! But it threw me off my game, and I was dragging badly until we stopped and got a chocolate croissant and another café con leche. Brian had started having trouble with his shoe; his insole kept shifting onto the side of his foot because his soles were so worn on one side. They were never intended to be his main Camino shoes and were fairly worn when he brought them. He was looking forward to tossing them when he reached Santiago as he had to stop periodically to take them off and fix his insole.

We'd sat down on a mossy wall to do just that when a Japanese woman stopped and leaned in to ask me "Peek-cher?" I thought she wanted me to take a picture of her and her husband, but when I said yes she plopped down beside me, put her arm around me, and pressed her cheek into mine. Her husband focused, snapped, and adjusted his location to get a better angle. I smiled, said "cheese," and wondered what they would tell their friends and family back home about me. People are funny!

Melide is a city of eight thousand people. It's known for its many restaurants serving the regional specialty, *pulpos*. There are many *pulperias* in the town, but I'd already had my octopus experience (yes, I count that one bite of Brian's). We found a tiny restaurant that turned out to be a jewel and had maybe one of the best hamburgers I've ever had in my life with a side of grilled vegetables with avocado sauce.

We had three more days of walking ahead, and I was ready to be finished. I was loving it, but it seemed like time to be done and yet we weren't. I was conscious of continuing to try to live in the moment, but it was more of a struggle than it had been. We'd now been walking for forty days.

Melide to Arzúa

Walking to Arzua we saw a donkey, many horses, cows, chickens, cats, and dogs. Rural Spain is different from rural America. America's spaciousness is rarely replicated, Spain looks older and more compact. It is. It's the Old World and it's beautiful and I wanted to remember this forever.

We passed by a tiny church and went to visit. In the doorway of the church was the grave of the man who had been the pastor for fifty-seven years, from 1905-1962. He was so beloved that they buried him right in front of the door, and everyone who enters the church walks over his tombstone. It's hard to imagine the changes he saw over that period. It would be even harder for him to imagine the changes that have taken place in the fifty-four years since then.

He was born in 1872 and was thirty-three years old when he became the pastor there, and lived to be ninety. He died right at the cusp of Vatican II, which brought such sweeping changes to the Catholic Church. I couldn't help but wonder about his life, about his ministry, about all the people whose lives he had touched. We too have pastored the same church for thirty-five years and this Camino sabbatical is a commemoration of that milestone. Seeing this man's grave made me grateful for him, and I felt a connection to him through our common stories and the mystical communion of saints. It made me grateful for our story, too, which is not over. Somehow this experience gave me a greater faith to walk trustingly into the future.

Arzua was another fairly big town, and we enjoyed walking the streets after checking into the hotel. We spent some time sitting in the square where a large memorial commemorated a famous local Spanish Civil War martyr. I know very little about the Spanish Civil War, but it was a tragic time for Spain with great suffering and the needless loss of many lives. I hate war.

We had a great dinner in the hotel that night—steak and potatoes and green beans. Two more days of walking. Excitement was growing.

Arzua to O Pedrouzo

We got an early start with headlamps. The sun is coming up so late, almost 9:00 here in extreme western Spain. Daylight savings time will come the week after we finish. We walked through woods a lot today. The leaves have mostly fallen off the trees and are dried and faded; the season has definitely changed. I saw jack o'lanterns, reminding me of home. The trees were green when we began, and it was summer; we have been away a long time.

I bought my first Camino souvenir in O Pedrouzo. I had lost an earring a few days earlier, a little green glass bead on a wire, earrings that I had worn the entire Camino. In O Pedrouzo I bought some blue scallop shell earrings because the scallop shell is the symbol of the Camino. I would wear them tomorrow as we marched into Santiago. Dinner was a salad with grilled goat cheese and risotto with vegetables.

That night I took a bath. Why? Because I could. Because we had a bathtub. It was warmer this evening, and I didn't need to take a bath to warm up. I thought about how many places I would loved to have had a hot bath and realized I was only taking one now because it somehow seemed like not taking a bath would have been a show of ingratitude. I laughed at myself with the awareness of my silly rationalization and again went to bed happy. Tomorrow was the last day of our Camino. Tomorrow we would arrive in Santiago. We were both excited and agreed to start even earlier the next day.

O Pedrouzo to Santiago

It was easy to jump out of bed when the alarm went off at 6:00. I might even have already been awake. We dressed quickly, the sense of anticipation energizing us more than usual, and walked out into the darkness of the night knowing there would be no light at all for a couple of hours.

It was surprisingly warm in the morning; we didn't need jackets. There was a sliver of a moon and a million stars twinkling overhead. We stopped to look at the stars and rejoice in them. Soon we entered into deep woods and deep darkness. The headlamps illuminated only a few steps ahead of us and were a reminder of what it is to walk by faith—unable to see the future, unable to see what lies ahead. But we saw enough; we saw what we needed to see and were making good progress.

I saw a piece of cardboard box laid out on the trail and as we went by realized someone had written a message on it. I said to Brian, "Hey, stop, I want to read this!" He was excited about moving, about getting there, and he grumbled a bit about going back. The sign said:

WELL DONE
You are nearly in
SANTIAGO
Congratulations!
Be Happy!
Smile!
Feliz!
Sonrisa!
Rock n Roll!
Buen Camino

   This made us both happy, and he was glad we'd stopped to read it. We passed a tent where someone was sleeping just off the path, and a sign that said the camper was looking for donations to get back home to Leicester, England. We then saw red taillights way off in the distance. I joked that it might be highway robbers, something that medieval pilgrims had had to watch out for. We finally approached a van pulled off the side of the room selling Camino souvenirs. In the euphoria of the day I bought a cheap Santiago bracelet for two euros that broke the next day and a Santiago ribbon to tie on my pack. Maybe they were highway robbers, the modern variety!

   It was warm and the air was humid and I noticed how well I could see my breath as the day began to dawn. As we were walking fast, I was breathing deeply and marveling on the huge billows of breath coming out of me. I thought about what I like to think of as "the breath within the breath." The breath of God, the spirit of God, inspiring, expiring. I breathe in deeply, as deeply and as fully as I can. Then I let it out. All the way out and then a little more. All the way in and then all the way out. Slowly.

Completely. Deliberately. Consciously. Bringing it inside me and then pushing it away, like ocean waves breaking on the beach. Slowly. Rhythmically. Repeatedly.

Concentrating on breathing, breathing with my whole self. Forgetting all else, nothing else matters. I breathe in—spirit? Inspiration? Inspiring spirit? Holy breath? Holy breath of God? Breathe it in. Let it go. Let it go? You can't hold on to God. You breathe God in, you let it go.

God is the breath within the breath. You breathe it in, you let it go, but something of God remains. Something is there nourishing you, sustaining you, uplifting you, strengthening you. A scientist might call it oxygen, but a mystic knows it is God. God is the thing that holds all things together; God is the one who gives life, who enlivens life.

I long to cling to God, to get God in my hot little hand and hold on tight. But what's an idol, but a God you can hold in your hand? I have to receive God as breath, as spirit, or as living water, flowing water which cannot be grasped. I have to take God in, not on my terms, but on God's.

And so I breathe in slowly, deliberately. I remember once again that I don't just live in a body but I am a body. I cherish and celebrate my body by breathing deeply and flooding all the parts of my body with all the God-source they need to live richly and fully. And then I let it go, knowing that letting go—not grasping and clinging—is just as important as breathing in.

These were my thoughts on that last day of the Camino as we walked through the darkness. I was aware that even when I don't see breath it's always there, just as God is always there even when I don't see him. God is present. Always.

I prayed for others as they came to my mind, for my niece recovering from her surgery and for friends and family back home. I thought about Sister Wendy Beckett, a hermit nun in

England who became famous as an art critic with her own BBC television show; I love her book, *Sister Wendy on Prayer*. She talks about absorbing the needs of the world and the people you are asked to pray for into yourself so that every prayer you pray encompasses every one of them. Every breath, every step can be a prayer. Keith Green sang "Make my life a prayer to you." I want to join the prayers of the world, for my life to be a prayer, to be a participant in the divine dance the Father, Son, and Holy Spirit are inviting me into.

The sun finally came out, and it was a beautiful day. Walking, walking, with such a sense of anticipation. I'd been looking forward to this not for forty days, but for four years!

But again, my expectation was a bit off. No, we did not "pop out of the woods" into the large plaza where the Cathedral of Santiago de Compestella stood. Maybe once upon a time a thousand years ago it had been like that. No, first we had to go past an airport. And some factories. Walking on asphalt. Through the suburbs. And into a fairly large developed city.

We finally arrived at the *Monte del Gozo*, the Mount of Joy, where early pilgrims had first glimpsed the Cathedral. But modern construction, including a monument commemorating the visit of Pope John Paul II, has obscured the view and we were still five kilometers from the Cathedral and the old city of Santiago. And it was here, at the Mount of Joy, that we actually lost the Camino for a bit, got off track for really the first time of the entire walk. We followed some people down a long sidewalk and realized after several minutes we were no longer on the Camino. We sheepishly turned around, walked back up a big hill, and shortcutted past some heavy construction equipment to where we could see pilgrims walking.

We joined them and in a short time were actually on busy city streets. We were in Santiago but not yet at our destination. We had another kilometer to walk through the city, and it was right here that we had a major breakdown. Yes, at the very end, at the last possible moment, we had our first fight of the Camino.

Like most fights, it was silly and senseless. It was a misunderstanding. It was two excited people who had different expectations, who have different ways of seeing life. It was over lunch. Food. Our customary *bocadillo* break. I was ready. I saw a little café and said, "Let's stop here and have our *bocadillo* break."

Brian said, "You're kidding, right?"

No, I wasn't kidding. It turns out that his excitement and euphoria caused him to want to get there as soon as he could. *Bocadillo* break was for all the other days. Not this one. We were practically there! Food could wait!

I had a very different perspective. Of course, today of all days we wouldn't want to go hungry. We should take our time, enjoy our last *bocadillo* break, stretch out the day, delay the gratification, and march triumphantly to the Cathedral with full and happy hearts. (And stomachs.)

I can't remember exactly what was said, but I got mad. We didn't eat. There were a few ugly words exchanged but just a few. I mostly seethed in silence. I was walking along, fuming to God, saying, "I can't believe this! Really? Really, God? We've walked four hundred and ninety-nine miles without a fight! What the heck? Really? Now?"

I wasn't blaming God, I wasn't saying this was God's fault, I just couldn't believe the Camino had been so perfect, we'd gotten along so well, it was such a special time for both of us and now, at the very end, I was so mad. And in my anger, in my questioning, I was surprised to hear God answer, words deep in my heart. I heard God say, "It's so you'll remember you're human."

I turned to Brian and said, "I can't walk into Santiago like this. I need to stop and sit and cool off. I'm really mad." In his defense, he'd already apologized. And now he stopped and we sat on a concrete wall in the busy city for several minutes while I tried to calm myself and cool off. It had been such a perfect pilgrimage, and I needed to tell myself that this wasn't going to ruin it. Yes, we were human. Humans have misunderstandings. They get over them and go on. We've had a great Camino, and this is just a little hiccup. It too can join all the other learning experiences of the Camino—learn to be quick to forgive, not to overdramatize but to accept our humanity and accept our differences, even to laugh at them. It turns out that I did not die of hunger that day. I let it go.

The streets were crowded. Santiago was a big city, but the Camino was clearly marked. There were other pilgrims making their way with their big packs and their hikers garb, easily differentiated from the business people with suits and briefcases sharing the sidewalks. We kept walking. The buildings became older as we entered the Old City, as sidewalks alongside heavily trafficked streets turned to narrow walkways. We finally walked down some long stairs and through a tunnel where musicians with bagpipes were playing and emerged onto the Plaza of Santiago. We had arrived.

Yes, we had arrived at a huge plaza flanking the Cathedral, our destination, the place where pilgrims had set their sights for over a thousand years, the place we'd been heading to for the past six weeks. And now that we were here, we weren't sure what to do. We wandered across the huge stone plaza to the opposite side and gazed back at the Cathedral. It was massive, ornate and beautiful and impressive, and I tried to ignore the scaffolding that now covered it, to acknowledge that it was only being preserved so that in the years to come people could continue to come on this spiritual pilgrimage. We looked for a place to sit down and headed for a big stone pillar to lean against. As we approached, a pilgrim reclining at the next pillar over with a big pack at his side slowly began to clap. He was applauding us, acknowledging our Camino. It was gratifying to know that someone else noticed. I smiled, took off my pack, put it on the ground, and sat down on the hard stones, resting my back against the pillar while Brian went over to talk to him. I found myself unable to talk, I just wanted to be quiet.

After a bit Brian came back. This man had also just walked in that day a little earlier than we had; he had walked from northern Germany and it had taken him four and a half months. He told Brian that we couldn't go in the church with our packs, which is what we'd intended to do. We would have to check into our lodging first, but before we did that we went to the Pilgrim office to get our *Compostellas*, our certificates of completion.

The office was a five-minute walk from the Cathedral square. I had envisioned long lines of pilgrims waiting to get their certificates, but there was no one in line. We walked right into the main office where several officials sat at a long counter. We each approached a different official who looked at our *credenciales* and questioned us for a few minutes before filling out our respective certificates. I regarded this as a business transaction while Brian found his experience quite emotional. As the official put the last stamp in his *credencial* he said to him, in English, "Your Camino is now finished," and handed him his completed *Compostella*.

When Brian heard the words, "Your Camino is finished," tears came suddenly to his eyes. He felt some sadness and found himself wondering if this was what would happen when his life was over—a pronouncement that it was finished. I, on the other hand, felt pensive and serious but not sad. I felt like everything was right and as it should be; I had a sense of completion and was a little surprised that I wasn't more emotional. As we met up at the exit I saw these words on the wall—"*Your night that lacked light has now become a torch of living faith.*" It was from the Codex Calixtinus, the 12th century pilgrim guide. Medieval pilgrims were guided by these words and I tried to ponder their meaning to me. They reminded me of a poem by Wendell Berry which becomes more meaningful in light of the Camino. Ah, such light!

> *We travelers, walking to the sun, can't see*
> *Ahead, but looking back the very light*
> *That blinded us shows us the way we came,*
> *Along which blessings now appear, risen*
> *As if from sightlessness to sight, and we,*
> *By blessing brightly lit, keep going toward*
> *That blessed light that yet to us is dark.*

Conclusion

A few years ago, I began practicing Centering Prayer, a form of Christian meditation. I like the verb "practicing" because it indicates two truths—one, that I am not very good at it, and two, the idea that it is a prayer "practice"—something I can decide to practice on a regular basis with the desire that it will help bring me closer to God, like an athlete working out on a daily basis to train his body to be stronger.

The big difference between Centering prayer and other forms of meditation is that it is a practice of continual surrender to God rather than an effort to do something. It is simple—providing a space for God to do God's work, rather than me doing mine. When I practice centering prayer, I usually set a timer, planning to spend a set amount of time (twenty minutes is recommended) doing absolutely nothing but sitting in the presence of God. It is fairly easy to quiet my body, but quieting my mind is another thing entirely; yet, that is my intention. It is a letting go of all thoughts, even thoughts about God. Of course I can't do this for long and catch myself repeatedly during each session thinking about all kinds of things. When I do, I simply let that thought go without judgment or self-recrimination; I surrender and again invite God in to the depths of my soul.

I breathe God in, knowing that breath and spirit are one and the same. I allow God into the hidden place deep within and trust that healing and restoration are taking place. I passively receive God's divine therapy. Yes, this is a passive prayer, a receiving prayer, not a matter of working up faith or even trying to say anything to God.

This is something that makes sense to me—God's divine therapy. If I were told that I had a deadly cancer and needed radiation, I would trustingly submit myself to that. I would willingly take the time to drive to the radiation center every day, lie down on a table and quiet myself, lying still for as long as it took. I probably wouldn't feel anything, but I would trust that something was happening—that radiation, an unseen force penetrating my body, was at work healing what was diseased, what was broken.

I practice Centering Prayer with this kind of faith. I trust that God is at work as I sit quietly, releasing each runaway thought as I become aware of it. My monkey mind was not accustomed to rest, but I feel myself becoming healthier as I continue to submit myself to God's divine therapy. All I really need to "do," all I really need to bring to this prayer is intentionality, my desire. My intention creates the space for God to work. My gift to God of the time it takes is the evidence of my faith. And I hear the echo of the voice of Jesus saying, "Your faith is making you well."

Yet, on the Camino, I didn't adhere to my usual prayer practices. There wasn't a conscious decision not to, but the Camino was so different than my regular life—rising in the morning to throw on clothes and begin our daily walk. The Camino gifted me the opportunity to practice prayer all day long. Every step became a prayer. Yes, I had read of that concept prior to the Camino, but on the Camino it became my experience. The practice of the presence of God, a phrase lifted from Brother

Lawrence, a humble fifteenth-century monk who is immortalized through that humility, became ever more real.

We spent three nights in Santiago enjoying the beautiful city. We attended two masses at the Cathedral and were able to experience the giant *botafumeiro* swinging through the air as incense filled the church. We saw people we'd met on the Camino and there was always a sense of family reunion when that happened—an exchange of stories and hugs. Brian saw a couple he'd never actually spoken to but remembered seeing several times and went out of his way to shake their hands and congratulate them. And then, after over six weeks of never moving faster than our feet could carry us (Godspeed?), we got in a taxi and rode to the airport to rent a car.

It felt strange to move so fast, and I felt myself initially resenting the ride. It was the beginning of re-entry into the real world, and I wasn't sure I was ready for that. We drove the road we'd walked a few days earlier, passing oncoming pilgrims who would be finishing their Caminos today, which thrilled my soul and made me want to honk and wave. I was able to resist reaching up over the seat to honk the horn as the driver probably would not have appreciated that! But I did roll down my window and wave wildly at the pilgrims, some of whom waved back.

At the airport we found the car rental window and waited behind a big guy who was leaning over the counter and clearly irritated over a mix-up with his rental. Wait, is that John, the Australian? The one we'd met up with in "Almost Atapuerca?" It was! We greeted him warmly and he was happy to see us too, except that he was pretty upset over the mix-up. I realized that irritations like this one, an all too common situation in real life, were one of the things that had made the Camino so delightful—the fact that we'd not had to deal with them. We got our car and offered him a ride anywhere he needed to go. He declined, determined to fight it out.

We drove off, headed for Finisterre. In recent years it has become popular to walk the extra hundred kilometers past Santiago to the ocean, the "end of the world." Neither of us had any desire to walk, but we wanted to see it. We spent a night in Finisterre, saw the sea, visited Muxia, and then drove back through Santiago to stay the night at an airport hotel before flying out the next morning to Barcelona.

As we retraced the last of our Camino steps, driving this time instead of walking, my heart was so filled with joy. A Bob Dylan line sprang to mind from *If You See Her Say Hello*, one of the songs that was on Brian's Camino playlist that we had often listened to while in our room at night. I spoke it aloud—"I know every scene by heart, they all went by so fast." I knew I would never forget this special time, this special gift we'd received.

We approached our hotel on a road through which the Camino trail weaved in and out. Standing at a crossing on her way to Santiago, I saw Betsy, one of the women we'd met ten long days ago at Hospital de la Cruz. She was on her way to finishing the Camino! She may have been a tortoise but undoubtedly a happy tortoise, and as we went by and I realized it was her, I almost told Brian to pull over so I could run back and give her a big hug of congratulations. But I didn't—seeing Betsy was a gift to me, and I was able to rejoice in her Camino and say a little prayer for her.

The next day we flew to Barcelona where we would spend four days before our return flight home. Our hotel was very near the *Basilica of Santa Maria del Mar*, a thirteenth-century church in Barcelona, and we visited there several times. On All Saints Day the church was packed with people milling about. I sat down on a pew about a third of the way back and looked around me. I had thought I would pray but I found myself saying, "It's too distracting to pray here, let me just sit here a while with you, God." I felt very comfortable just sitting with God and aware that the usual sense of self-accusation and "shoulding" myself that I'd always known was curiously absent. I felt lighter somehow, as if I'd shed a heavy burden. I was no longer carrying a pack with me, but I was to understand later I'd shed something much heavier while on the Camino. These were my thoughts as I sat with God that morning in the church.

I looked around me, surrounded by people everywhere. People with cell phones, milling about, taking pictures, sitting, reading, tweeting. People crossing themselves, genuflecting, or merely pausing for just a minute. Indistinguishable whispers, low voices, occasional louder voices, Spanish, French, German, English. Frequent shushing--Sssshhh! The sounds of shuffling feet, the scrape of chairs, coughing, all echoing in the cavernous room. I see all these people you have created, Lord, and I feel your heart of love for each one. It makes me love them too.

People in a church. Maybe they've just come to see an ancient building, to admire the architecture, but they all slow down, they crane their heads upward, they stop, and surely are aware they're encountering something bigger than themselves. The space is inviting—Gothic architecture with its soaring arches and vaulted ceilings. The decoration is simple and unpretentious, and the altar is plainly and tastefully adorned with white floral arrangements. The centerpiece is a small statue of Madonna and Child in pastel, and to the side is the banner I've seen in churches all across Spain, announcing and celebrating Pope Francis' Year of Mercy. Oh Lord, we really need your mercy now, as much as ever; mercy seems to be in such short supply.

I see a woman with a walker and brightly patterned hippie pants make her way to the altar, pausing to reflect. Right behind her is a young man dressed hip-hop style, earbuds in place, his gait seeming to move with the music only he can hear, but he's here, before you, Lord.

A beam of sunlight is streaming through a high open window--a spotlight that people stumble into and look up, surprised. A little girl twirls in it, laughs. Her dad, watching, then takes his turn, delighting her with his own twirl. It makes me smile. Then I realize it has made you smile, too, God.

The huge cathedral is lined with small chapels, and one near me features Jesus as the Good Shepherd. A man and woman sit side by side in this tiny chapel, their heads bowed, their lips moving silently. Her hands are open in her lap, she is wearing a blue dress. I don't know them, but I know they have a story, and that you are at work in their lives just as you are in mine, God. Bless them, be with them, and grant them your peace, dear Lord.

And then I see a woman approaching the altar, wearing conservative Muslim dress, a long black coat and a headscarf, sunglasses pushed up on her head. She stops and stands quietly, gazing. I feel surprised and my heart quickens a bit. God, I hope she feels welcome here! She finally turns and walks away. Oh my sister, I pray people treat you well, that you might know the love of God and the love of those you live amongst.

A handicapped woman in an electric wheelchair struggles to light a candle before the chapel of Christ on the cross before finally turning and asking someone nearby for help. A woman is quick to respond, and then the two are quiet together in contemplation. Lord, give them both whatever it is they need today.

And then I realize it's time to leave, but I've so enjoyed sitting here this morning with God, and I think God has enjoyed it, too.

Six months later, I think about the Camino every day. Brian and I talk about the Camino often. We both acknowledge we were profoundly changed. Journaling through every day of the Camino, reliving it, has helped me to further understand and process it. God accomplished a work of grace in me, in us, while we walked the Camino. I ponder and marvel over this—I'm astonished and so very grateful. I see the changes in me, I feel them. I feel them every day. There is so much more peace in my life. I see the changes in Brian, too—big ones. We long to go back and do it over again, at the same time acknowledging that it won't be the same.

Yes, I do know every scene by heart, they all went by so fast. I'm thankful, so thankful. Thankful for the Camino and for the journey of my life, which continues. The Camino, through the allegory for life that it is, gave me a chance to see my life from a different perspective. It's hard to see your life when you are immersed in it. The Camino allows you to step back and see life less subjectively. Paulo Coehlo says, "Life always teaches us more than the Camino de Santiago does, but we don't have much faith in what life teaches us." I am listening better to my life after walking the Camino. My "Buen Camino" is helping me to live an even better life today.

Six months later, what are some of the things I have come to understand? What are some of the soul deposits that have taken root in me since I walked the Camino? I understand that the Camino was a place of rest for me. How can I continue on in the strength of that rest? I must ponder this.

I find myself much kinder and gentler to myself since the Camino. It's not a selfish thing to take care of yourself, but an attitude of allowing God to care for you, receiving rivers of living water into your soul so that living water can flow out to others, so you have something to give others. I am far less self-critical; that accusing voice in my head that has always told me I wasn't good enough has been greatly silenced, and I don't miss it. I am amazed, I marvel, worship God, and continue to ponder this.

I rejoice in how "perfect" my experience was, that everything just seemed to come together, but know that it doesn't mean God particularly favored us or loved us more. If things had gone differently, I'd just have a different story. I would find meaning and goodness in it and would give thanks to God as well. What if we weren't able to finish? I pray I would find meaning in that too. This is a big paradigm shift. Pondering, with thankfulness.

I thank God for my blisters. I never thought I would find myself writing a sentence like that. God gave me the opportunity to face one of my biggest fears right off, thank you very much! I learned that pain is amplified when I am afraid of more pain. And that pain in my leg as I walked along the path of crosses? I'm still mystified. But I feel closer to God as a result of the conversation I had with Jesus as I attempted to find him in that pain. Jesus wasn't offended by my honesty but accepted me as I am. I realize now that was prayer.

Prayer is such a hard word to define, but the goal of all prayer is to find yourself in the presence of God. I'm much more relaxed about what "qualifies" as prayer these days. I've returned to my daily practice of a morning liturgy and scripture—these are the practices that open my spirit to experiencing God. Sitting with God in the church in Barcelona was prayer, and I left that moment impacted by God's presence.

I had thought my experience at the Cruz de Ferro where I laid down the burden I'd carried with me from home, the little yellow stone that represented my false self, was anti-climactic. It didn't seem dramatic or very emotional, but I was to understand later that I really was deeply changed as a result. I did leave something behind there, parts of me that were false—deeply ingrained ways of thinking that seemed to keep me fragmented, perpetually uptight and frustrated because life wasn't perfect.

A few years before, while meditating on the Twenty-third Psalm, a vivid image had come to mind contemplating "a table set before me in the presence of my enemies." I had imagined a beautiful picnic feast set on a blanket on the ground in a clearing in the woods, with fine crystal and china place settings. God was inviting me to sit down and enjoy the feast he had prepared, but I was reluctant, instead focused on "enemies" I could see lurking behind nearby trees.

Those "enemies" were my unsolved problems, and they always seemed to be there. I imagined myself hearing God's invitation to sit down and enjoy the feast, but I responded, "No, not until you get rid of those enemies that are all around me!"

God's only response was to repeat the invitation. I knew God was asking me to live in the moment, to embrace and love what is right now, to trust God enough that I could be at peace and live with unsolved problems. But that wasn't an easy thing to do, not at all. It so went against the grain of the way I'd always approached life.

As I've prayed that psalm almost daily for the past several years, I continually heard that same invitation from Jesus. Hundreds of times. Can I let go of a need for control—just like that, just let it go? I realize now that something internally shifted in me when I laid down that little yellow stone, and the "slow work of God" finally prevailed in a very anti-climactic way.

Am I saying I don't still freak out sometimes when faced with a problem? Of course not. But I am a lot less uptight about problems. Sometimes I simply accept them, sit down and enjoy the feast that is present for me today, and trust that God will be there tomorrow when the problem actually has to be faced.

Walking across Spain I experienced the Camino as a living entity, a thin place, a river I would enter, a flow I was magnetically drawn to each day. I trusted that the Camino would provide what I needed. I got corrected a couple of times, "You mean that God will provide what you need through the Camino," but in truth, that seemed to minimize the qualities that the Way itself possessed.

Medieval pilgrims went on the journey believing that the bones of a dead apostle had power that would provide forgiveness, healing, miracles. Maybe Jesus would say to them, "Be it done to you according to your faith." Their faith made them well. They received forgiveness, healing, and miracles on the Camino. People of the Enlightenment tend to be skeptical of such things. But the Camino grew my faith. I do have faith in sacraments, in the bread and wine, in the Eucharist meal. That faith continues to enlarge. I believe not just in a spiritual God, but in a God who is able to come to us in a physical way through this created world, through tangible, material things which the spirit of God mysteriously indwells. This is my Father's world! The Camino is definitely a thin place.

It's a place where the veil between spirit and earth sometimes disappears, a place suffused with the presence of the holy and sacred. You quickly learn that you mustn't try to make anything happen, you must only stay attentive and listen, trusting the Camino will provide exactly what you need. This is a mystery, but God is an even greater mystery. We will never comprehend God, we can only experience God, worship God, and wonder at God. I must continue to ponder this.

As I get some distance from the Camino, I see it even more clearly as a metaphor for all of life. The beginning, over the Pyrenees and through wine country, symbolizes to me the delight of childhood—learning, making discoveries, everything new, shiny, and bright. But then we come to the Meseta, where we enter adulthood, the real world where most of us spend most of our lives—raising children, building homes, struggling to make it, figuring out what it's all about. This is the Meseta—that middle section of life, that sometimes boring, sometimes tedious section of life—but we realize in hindsight how beautiful it all was and that we wouldn't have skipped it for anything! Cheating? Skipping it? You're not cheating anyone but yourself! In fact, you'd give anything to go back and live it all over again, wishing you could do it with the knowledge you've now learned. You can't.

And then you leave the Meseta and cross more mountains. You realize the end is nearer, but that's it's really just a beginning. That section of life is, hopefully, mostly still ahead for me. It's a mystery, but a mystery I now approach more trustingly, more willingly, surrendering myself to the purposes of God. Oh, so much to ponder.

It is good to have an end to journey toward,

but it is the journey that matters, in the end.

Ernest Hemingway

Afterword

By Brian Zahnd

*I*t was a long walk across Spain—the best days of our lives. We knew it while we were doing it. Even when we were beset with blisters and worn down by fatigue, we would turn to one another and say, "This is the best thing we've ever done." While walking thousand-year-old paths made holy by the feet of millions of pilgrims, we found respite "far from the madding crowd" of modernity. For forty days and forty nights our lives were reduced to the blessed simplicity of walking from town to town, from church to church, from shelter to shelter, always moving a bit closer to Santiago. We didn't dart here and there, back and forth in a frenzy; we didn't speed through the world in cars, trains, and planes; we just moved steadily westward, no faster than foot speed. And with the simplicity and the slowing down came that which we miss most in our high-speed, high-tech, high-stress age: Peace.

We had come to the Camino to escape the quadrennial madness that falls upon America during presidential elections. We had come to the Camino for our first sabbatical in thirty-five years of ministry. We had come to the Camino in hope of finding healing for our over-wrought souls. And on the Camino we found all we were looking for and more. It's not often that a much-anticipated experience exceeds our expectations, but the Camino de Santiago was better than we had dared to hope. It was a gift from God; a five-hundred mile walk deep into the grace of Christ.

As it became known that we planned to walk the Camino, people who had already had their own Camino contacted us; they were as eager to tell us of their experience as we were to gain what advice we could. Over time I noticed that these Camino veterans tended to say the same three things in their own way:

1. It's harder than you think.
2. You will love it.
3. It will change you.

Today, six months after our arrival in Santiago, I can say that all three prophecies were precisely true. It *was* harder than I anticipated—as Peri's story makes clear. And I *did* love it. Even when I had seventeen blisters I was aware that I loved the privilege of being a pilgrim on this wonderful journey. And, most importantly, I believe the Camino *has* changed me. I found a peace on the Camino that I'm still consciously aware of today.

Over those five hundred miles I shed a layer of skin—a layer that was too easily blistered by anxiety. At Cruz de Ferro I laid down a burden I have not retrieved—I left it at the base of an ancient iron cross and there it will remain. Those long walks through the lovely mountains of the Pyrenees, the vineyards of Navarra, the plains of the Meseta, and the wooded hills of Galicia brought me to a new place of calm and contentedness. This was an answer to prayer. The Camino was a forty-day, five-hundred mile prayer, and with the Amen offered in the Cathedral of Santiago I found a new depth of the peace of God which surpasses all understanding. Thank you, Camino. Thank you, Peri. Thank you, Jesus.

Buen Camino.

65204445R00125

Made in the USA
Lexington, KY
04 July 2017